ALL THAT MATTERS

By Jean Anderson

All That Matters

Dedication

This book is dedicated to Mark Bratlie,
who brought love, laughter and a new world to me.

And to Jill and Karen,
delights of the next generation.

CONTENTS

Preface

The experiences in these essays and the writing of them span decades of my life. The chapters are not in absolute chronological order so they can be read individually.

My intent is to share the pathways to peace that I've found while winding through the ups and downs of a life filled with many joys, some sorrows, a few mysteries, and everything that lies in between.

I began weaving the poems of my late husband Mark into the pages when I realized that his thoughts were a colorful counterplay to my own.

In the end, what matters for me is this — I want to love with some abandon and to choose hope and grace as my companions.

Welcome to the world, I told myself;
I hope I know a blessing when I see one.

– Kathleen Norris, "Dakota: A Spiritual Geography"

CHAPTER 1

Waking Up to the World

Stepping Out

It began long ago on a country coastal road in South Carolina after a humiliating word or two was tossed my way during a spur-of-the-moment football scrimmage.

"You've got a lot to move there, sister." Leaving the game, I looked down at my body and realized that, yes, I did have a lot to move. I started walking. The first steps turned into a mile, and that mile has turned into many more.

The miles have sped by. I walk quickly and very rarely stroll. I've mused, moaned, and muttered. I've prayed, cried, and laughed. I've walked on gravel roads, dirt roads, rutted roads, snow-packed roads, and no roads – on icy sidewalks, wet sidewalks, leafy sidewalks, city sidewalks, and village lanes. I've walked up and down hills, in fields, across ditches, over beaches, around lakes, and across frozen swamps with snowshoes. I've done a lot of walking. The miles have passed by, and the more I walk the happier I become.

Walking has been a heart opener and a wise teacher. Once, in a quiet rage over a long-brewing stew with a friend, I stomped around a lake, cussing and wishing him the worst. I called it "prayer." All of a sudden – in the midst of my stomping and storming – I heard a voice: "*If you would wish the best for him, only the best can happen to you.*" The voice startled me and I realized I was no longer angry.

Another time, deeply sorrowed at my brother's sudden change in health, I set out on my way sobbing. Midway through the park, I noticed three little boys bent over, quivering with energy, chattering, and pointing. One looked over, spotted me, and ran up with a tiny jar covered with a screen and a bumble bee inside: "Look, look, what we've found!" Yes, inside was a golden bumble bee. Then my world of sorrow cracked open to reveal the joy hidden inside.

I've learned to love weather and all that it brings. I've even amused myself. One morning, eager to see the world after a wild winter storm, I set out. But the ice was so slick, I slipped and fell four times in the first five minutes.

Luckily, before falling once again, I came to my senses and slid home.

My walking has helped me see the world and my good fortune more clearly. It started with the physical – a throw-away comment that set me on a course thinking about my body – but it transformed me in other ways. Walking set me on a course to let go of burdens, to rejoice, and to change – just as nature does.

Variations on the Theme of Light

It was two months after my brother David died, in midwinter, and still the deepest, darkest part of the year. A long-planned trip with two of my friends to another friend's home was ahead, but as I thought about it, a dread came over me.

I'd carved out big days in my calendar for the get-together. My heart had leapt when I turned the calendar pages to see the empty space that had been created. But my leaping heart was for the empty space. I had an insatiable craving and a gnawing hunger for it to remain just that way … a wide-open space. It seemed the best way to honor my favorite brother, my only brother, David Lawrence Anderson. And so, I canceled my trip. Then for five days, early in the morning, I sat cozied in the love seat that gave me the perfect outlook on the dawning of the day. For several hours early each morning I listened, watched, and prayed. One day the progression from dark to dawn surprised me. In the midst of that darkness of night were houses of beautiful colors — white, rose, blue, and yellow.

All during those long hours of darkness the lovely colors had been present but simply hidden to my eyes. Now I could see them clearly. Along with the dawn that day, a healing in me was born.

~ ~ ~

If I took the "holy" out of holiday, my hands-down favorite would be the Summer Solstice, June 21st. Each year my goal on that day is to be out in the country with a clear sightline to the setting sun. How I love to watch that giant ball of glory slip and slide from its noon high down, down, down into the western sky. Standing alert and at attention until the last glimmer of evening light fades away, I always wonder, "Where is it going? Can I follow?"

~ ~ ~

On my first morning in Sweden, I awoke cheered by a good night's sleep and the light that greeted me. It must be about 6:00 or 6:30, I thought as I glanced at the clock. I took one look and then my head swiveled back in a double take. 3:17 a.m. What? Is this clock working? What is that mysterious light doing out in the middle of the night? Am I dreaming? It was a glow I had never seen before in the night hours. I got up and took a picture.

And yes, it was a true awakening. I was in Sweden, my ancestral homeland, a place of all-night-long summer light.

~ ~ ~

My bathroom break often wakes me in the middle of the night. Yet, on the last few nights meandering my way back to bed, I wonder which neighbor left the big bright yard light on. I shield my eyes, avoiding contact because I know that if I look at it, I'll totally wake up.

But last night, after taking my dive into bed after such a break, I realized the light is spread out over my bed, just like sunlight during the day. And then it dawned on me — the neighbor who left the big light on is God. We might call it moonlight, but it's God's light!

No wonder light is described as illuminating. Moonlight … for the past couple of nights I've been shading my eyes from the full moon. Now instead of shielding my eyes, I want to be awake to lie in the light and gather up its glowing rays.

And what about spiritual light? We can be bathed in that too . . . or we can avert our eyes from it. The light is always there. And it keeps shining. Sometimes with great fullness. I wonder how often I recognize it and open myself up to it.

The sweetness of last night, with its delicious discovery of the full moon's light, and my immediate change of heart, opened me. This recognition brings sweet joy to my face. I thought of how I've always pushed away light at night as bothersome and intrusive. And yet not more than five hours ago, what was one minute bothersome, was the next minute bringing me quiet glee. It was the same light source. Only after a moment did I name it differently, and then it became a thing of marvel.

There can be dark times in our world. During these seasons of darkness, we're called to bring light — to be a light to others.

One passage from Scripture reads: "You are the light of the world. A city on a hill cannot be hidden. Neither do people light a lamp and put it under a bowl. Instead, they put it on its stand, and it gives light to everyone in the house. In the same way, let your light shine before all …". (Matthew 5:14-15)

Ah, here is our calling! For yes, we're each called to be, in our own individual way, a light in the world. We're created with a light - a spirit within. How will you do it? How will you be a light?

A Cure for the Busy-ness Disease

I may have been too busy — running to one more meeting, event, or social gathering. For the umpteenth time when I introduced myself or greeted someone and asked, "How are you?" the same response came back, "Oh, I'm so busy."

As I looked to confirm the names on various event badges, I chuckled to myself and thought, we could skip the name tags that read, "Hi, I'm Bill," and move right on to badges that would instead declare, "Hi, I'm Busy."

The announcement of busy-ness is being made so frequently these days that I'm beginning to think of it as our newest addiction. We've even gone beyond busy — we're now "crazy busy" — and "rest" has become the newest four-letter word.

What is this crazy busy stuff? Busy, busy, busy. Say yes, do more, go faster, commit more energy, occupy more time. We're so in the habit of running — for family, work, self, church, social gatherings, and community events — that taking our ease has become downright un-American.

I too used to be a proponent of the busy school of life. Now, I am a proponent of a different kind of busy-ness. I'm busy trying to set aside one day of full retreat for myself every few weeks — a Sabbath Day, or Day of Rest, as it used to be called. No emails, no driving, no grocery shopping, no phone calls, no web-lounging. On that day, I aim to go nowhere except where my own two feet or two pedals will take me. Among other things, I try to see that they will take me to a hammock or a couch or a lawn for a refreshing snooze or some serious cloud watching.

It turns out initially at least, that this resting is hard work! It's no easy task to take it easy. And I know I'm not alone in this thought.

A friend of mine who has multiple sclerosis was having difficulty with movement and balance. Since I knew that her life, as well as her ability to be busy, depends on being able to rest, I asked her if she'd been able to get some. "Oh! I'm not one for rest," she responded, "I've never been able to rest. I always need to be busy working on something."

Hers was the type of response that I find tough to combat. I know that some of us are Type As and do need constant stimuli; but still, in her case, *her ability to be busy depends on being able to rest*. This spurred me on to realize that I needed to encourage her in an entirely different way. So I said, "Oh, I was using the wrong language. I meant to say, have you been able to work at resting? You can tell yourself and others that you're busy – it's just that you're busy taking it easy." She laughed and said, "That's a much better way to look at it."

When I first started trying to explore having a quiet day, or a rest zone, it was like a deep, dark, scary tunnel, and I would try to fill it up with tasks, phone calls, and invitations. It wasn't until a few hours had passed that I could move through all the disconnected in my head and finally connect back with the calm inside me. Then the great bonuses of this retreat began to surface — whimsical imaginings, new ideas, rejuvenated relationships, and fresh energy to solve problems.

But finding the time to retreat *is* hard work. I have to schedule it out, far in advance, just like a dental appointment. I figure it to be an appointment with myself.

Friends have said to me, with a bit of incredulity and doubt in their voice, "How do you do that? How can you find time to take a day off?" I wondered too, and then I realized that I was simply using that old stock phrase: "Just say no."

"Can you go to the movies tomorrow night?" "No." "Are you available for dinner?" "No, I'm not." "Would you like to go on a trip over the weekend?" "No, I can't." Of course, in most instances, I would love to do those things. But, having scheduled out my retreat days several months ahead, I know which days I can and can't be available for the outward part of my life.

My first real appreciation of the other side of busy-ness came when I was forced by an illness to retreat from my usual pace. As a result of the treatment for the illness, my get-up-and-go had gotten up and gone. Nonetheless, I ached to regain the hectic life I'd had before. Illness will do that to you. You'd give anything to go back to life as it was. But this experience also made me understand the value of deep rest.

After that, I began to rest with abandon. And now, many years later, long cured of that physical disease, I find myself also cured of the disease of always being busy. All it takes is a commitment to one Sabbath Day every few weeks.

And the amazing thing is that this time of doing "nothing" often turns out to be the most productive time of all – not only in the sense of ideas I can envision and problems I can solve, but also in the gift of solace for my soul.

A Slower Pace

By Mark Bratlie

Quick, quick, hurry, hurry,
time is passing with a flurry –
Things to do, no time to linger,
life is caught up in a wringer.
But whoa, whoa, let's slow the pace –
life need not be an all-out race.
What of life's gifts that pass on by
as treasures lost to make one cry?
Seasons' colors and nature's beauty
ask for time for us to see.
A slower pace allows some focus
as life's wonders beg for notice –
A leaf, a cloud, a summer shower,
a rainbow's arc, a full moon's power,
A child's giggle, a lover's sigh,
a sweet embrace, a refreshing cry,
An open mind, a relaxing breath,
a calm acceptance of life and death.
The invitation is ours to ponder
as we focus on a life of wonder.

CHAPTER 2

The Farm

The Man with His Head in a Tree

Picking up the ringing phone, I heard my dad's lilting Swedish voice, "The light bulb just came on. I was walking to the seed plant when I thought, *tree farm — that's it!"*

And so began my return to the land where I'd grown up. For years I'd longed to work on the land, but the trick for us was finding just how to do that. My dad and I had explored many options. We spoke of a vegetable farm or a flower farm or a native grass seed site, but it wasn't until the phone rang that night that the right idea gelled for both of us – tree farm. My return to the land began.

Years later, when our evergreen trees were large enough for sale, I left visiting husband and wife, Daniel and Sarah, to look through the rows of trees on their own. I'd learned to leave people alone as they considered, talked, and tussled about which trees to buy.

A few minutes later, I wandered back to find a most unusual sight — there was Daniel with his head tilted deep inside the branches of a tree. I paused. He paused. He pulled his head out of the tree. Perhaps it was the questioning look on my face that led him to say, "I was listening to the tree." And then, "I play in the symphony orchestra."

I came to understand more later. Because he was the tympani player for the Fargo-Moorhead Orchestra and a Professor of Percussion at a local college, he was turning his head toward the innards of the tree to hear its subtle sounds and rhythms.

Daniel wasn't alone in listening to trees. Paul J. Christiansen, choral conductor and composer at Concordia College, while on a choir tour in Norway, was walking in the woods with students. He suddenly stopped and pointed to a grove of trees. Cocking his head and listening, he said: "That's how I want my altos to sound."

Clearly, musicians have a remarkable knack for listening — to music in all sorts of spheres.

In my world, is there a better way to choose a tree than to lean in and listen to it? Not likely! And so, my favorite customer became the man with his head in the tree.

A Flight of Delight

The phrase "A Flight" brings many types of flights to mind. There's Orville and Wilbur Wright's airplane flight, the Biblical flight out of Egypt, and flights of wine.

Last summer I witnessed the best flight ever. Upon hearing from a farm neighbor that an enormous hailstorm hit during the night, totaling their two cars and damaging roofs, siding, and windows, my husband Mark and I drove quickly out to the small acreage of land where we have a dazzling 24-foot octagonal glass gazebo. My thoughts were on the glass gazebo. I fully expected to find it scattered in shards on the ground.

Had I been driving alone, in a wild dash across the grassy field road, I would have missed the most amazing flight imaginable.

"Look, look!" Mark cried. I hit the brakes, fully expecting to see some devastating sight of damage. I braced for the worst. My gaze followed his outstretched arm to the trees in the shelter belt. From one of the trees arose dozens and dozens of monarch butterflies. Their bright orange wings painted the sky as they flew. They dipped, swayed, and floated in the morning light.

And our gazebo escaped with nary a nick from the hailstorm.

The monarch butterflies? They too escaped — but not before leaving me transformed. Here I was imagining destruction, yet instead I saw the butterflies glorious in their flight. How quickly my world changed.

Losing the Land

The land in the Red River Valley is flat. Flatter than flat. It was formed from an ancient glacial lake bottom. So flat and open that you can see for miles. That's part of its charm. It's also one of the hazards of living here. The Red River flows north carrying melting ice and snow from areas and states to the south. In the spring this water threatens to overflow the Red River into the cities and towns of North Dakota and Minnesota. It can become a recipe for a natural disaster: massive spring floods.

The Red River's worst flood since 1826 was in 1997. That year a wild winter of 11 blizzards with 10 feet of snow melted rapidly in the spring, causing a catastrophic flood to demolish downtown Grand Forks, a city to our north. Over 50,000 people were evacuated from Grand Forks and East Grand Forks, the largest evacuation, at that time, of an American city since Atlanta was evacuated during the Civil War.

It left Fargo-Moorhead a sandbagged, waterlogged, and exhausted city. Fargo escaped enormous devastation because of a fluke of nature, plus 12,000 volunteers who filled more than one million sandbags. But what we didn't escape was the fright of just barely missing a monumental flood. Then twelve years later, in 2009, the region was hit by another massive flood. This time volunteers filled over 2 million sandbags, but even so, the flood demolished many homes and businesses. This flood left behind a lesson: protect the cities of Fargo-Moorhead. At all costs.

The plan began. Over a decade, what has become known as the Fargo-Moorhead Diversion Project took shape. It's the largest and first of its kind ever undertaken by the U.S. Corp of Engineers: a joint public and private project of the federal government, North Dakota, Minnesota, several cities, towns and counties within the two states, and private contractors.

This flood control project included a 30-mile diversion channel, and the crossings of 3 railroads, 2 pairs of interstate highways, and 12 county roads. There was river rerouting, water retention plans, gated control outlets, dikes and dams. It also meant the wholesale removal of homes and farmsteads.

The initial cost was projected at 1.8 billion in 2014. By 2023, the cost had ballooned to 3.4 billion.

While one can't help but be astonished and amazed by the engineering feat, many people who were working and living in the impacted areas had grave reservations about some of the rationales for claiming this land. Some of the land had never flooded and is known to be some of the richest farmland in the world.

Much of the anger grew because of the claim, once stated by the Mayor of Fargo at a community meeting with the Governor of Minnesota: "But Fargo has to have room to grow." Being bound by other cities to the west and east, and having limited growth potential to the north, the only way for Fargo to grow was to allow land to the south that historically had been in a flood plain to be included and protected by this massive diversion plan.

The need for flood control was real. The need for protected land so Fargo could grow was also real. However, the issue of growth became hidden and muted under the claim of flood protection. This was unfortunate and it stoked resentment.

I was one of those people affected by the project. As a Fargo homeowner who had participated in sand-bagging efforts, I embraced the need for flood protection. As a small landowner in Minnesota, I was also angered by the slow response to address valid concerns of Minnesota landowners who were about to lose valuable farmland. Land that had never flooded. We Minnesotans weren't a happy bunch. It felt like we were being railroaded.

Of course, being railroaded began long ago in our country. The railroads claimed native land in the 1800s and continued to break up communal tribal lands for the benefit of white settlers. In the 1950s and 1960s, the interstate highway system that was constructed through major American cities destroyed African-American neighborhoods. The only difference this time was that landowners were being compensated, but the questions remained: *Was this the best and most just plan, and was the compensation adequate?*

Over time, the farmers and landowners in Minnesota pressed for better results. Because Moorhead sits 4' higher in elevation than Fargo, and Moorhead did not need the diversion as much as Fargo, Minnesota residents did not want the diversion on their side of the river.

It was North Dakota that would benefit most from the Diversion Project and so the State of Minnesota sued for stronger outcomes for its citizens. As a result, the southern earthen embankment that would hold back overflow flood waters was relocated, saving thousands of acres of Minnesota farmland and a small town from intentional flooding.

Also included in the negotiated agreement was crop insurance for the farmers. The Diversion also took responsibility for removal of the debris that would be left by the flooding.

Farmers had a grave concern that timely spring planting might be impossible, given the flooding and the time necessary for the land to dry out enough so that heavy equipment could be used to remove the remaining debris. All these additional critical changes made the Project *slightly* more palatable.

At some point you have to accept change. Right or wrong, ‘progress’ occurs, and some people benefit and some don't. The Diversion was finalized, and the buyouts of farmsteads, buildings, and land began.

I was lucky. My stake in the loss of land was minor compared to many of my Minnesota neighbors, but still it was significant. Seven miles south of Moorhead, on the very edge of the Red River, stands the log cabin that my great-grandparents built when they immigrated from Sweden in 1869. It had never flooded. Amazing. The Diversion is claiming it, but because it's on the National Register of Historic Buildings, it won't be demolished but moved 34 miles to a new location.

Next in line for the Diversion's claim was the Clara Cemetery, a mile south of the log cabin. It's where my ancestors and family - parents, sister, brother, and my husband Mark — are buried.

Among the 11 cemeteries facing new flood risk because of the Diversion Project, a news headline read, "Clara Lutheran Cemetery faces the greatest risk." Engineers recommended building a dike 8 feet high around it, but cemetery and church people dismissed that idea, saying "No, we'd feel like we were in a swimming pool when visiting the cemetery."

A compromise was reached and the proposed 8-foot dike was lowered to 4 feet to protect the historic cemetery.

A 5-bedroom farmstead built in 1905 where my dad was born and where he and my mom raised our family faced its own buyout. Also included in this buyout was the crop seed cleaning and conditioning facility that my dad built. Yet on the same morning that an appraiser came to my property, our seed plant was being demolished. It was quietly ironic. In the background as we walked, I could see and hear the wrecking ball taking the seed plant down.

Adjacent to the farmstead is what my family has always affectionately called “The 80”. Eighty acres of farmland that’s been in our family for generations. It’s the land where I’ve walked the fields and spent days pulling weeds. A portion — 23 acres — of this land has been claimed by the Diversion because the southern earthen embankment of the flood containment structure will be built there. We now less affectionately refer to it as “The 57”.

And the final loss? My property. In between the farmstead where I grew up and the 80 acres, was a 6-acre site where my dad and I started and managed a tree farm,

Trees in the Valley. Again, land in the family for generations. Over seven years, my husband Mark and I turned it into our "lake place without a lake." Loved and cared for by many. Now a buyout for the benefit of the Diversion.

And so, here I stood. Needing to accept the changes. Needing to move on. How was I to do it?

Acceptance came like it frequently does — with the passage of time and with attention. It took several years for the Diversion plan to be approved, so I had time to come to terms with what would eventually happen. Once when playing a game designed to help with quandaries of life, I'd pulled 3 cards meant to guide me on my search for peace with the buyouts: *trust, openness, birth*. I held these continually in my mind's eye.

To prepare for the appraisal that would put a value on my property for the buyout, I was working hard to get everything in tiptop shape. The appraisal was a part of the required buyout to compensate those losing land and buildings to the Diversion Project. I was having trouble explaining to others what I was doing, so I started putting down on paper all the effort I'd put into preparation.

I pulled,
pushed,
planted,
pondered,
and prayed.

I carried,
carted,
cleared,
and clipped.

I mowed, sitting.
I mowed, standing.
I mowed in shelterbelts
in 90-plus degree heat and humidity.

I lugged,
lifted,
and loaded.

I hoed,
hosed,
hefted,
and hauled.

I stretched,
strained,
stooped,
swept,
scrubbed,
squatted,
and swatted.

I washed,
  weeded,
  walked,
  waited,
  wandered,
  and whacked.

I remembered.
I mourned.

I'd worked hard over six weeks' time to prepare for the appraisal. I came to grips with the loss of my land – the loss of my beloved country oasis.

It's Never Enough, Is It?

That was my thought when I read that "ND Seeks to Join Lawsuit to Decide Who Owns Riverbed." (*The Forum* headline, Wednesday, May 4th, 2022). The riverbed in question is the "bed of the historic Missouri River that flows inside the boundaries of the Fort Berthold Reservation."

Never mind that an 1851 treaty with the Mandan, Hidatsa, and Arikara tribes "gave" the tribes the land. Never mind that the tribes were the original inhabitants and trustees of the land until the reservation borders were set by the U.S. government.

Now that the reservation land in dispute includes 255 oil and gas wells, with mineral lease royalties currently estimated to exceed $116 million, the state of North Dakota has decided that they are the rightful owners. It seems there's always some way to justify greed.

The white man — or white society — has a wretched tradition of making promises or treaties and then breaking them.

I say, "Honor the treaty."

Prairie Spirit
By Mark Bratlie

I gaze on vast spaces
not empty
not disturbing
but settled and inviting

I gaze on vistas of stillness
not rushing
not anxious
but calm softness

I gaze on distant treelines
not unruly
not intrusive
but green contentment

I gaze on endless sky
not threatening
not overwhelming
but bluer than blue

I gaze with awe and wonder
as my inner spirit expands
not to compete
not to fill
but to be with
with vastness
with stillness
with Prairie Spirit

CHAPTER 3

Paying Attention

The Treasure Outside the Pantry Door

Is there anything better than a big kitchen pantry? Oh, the storehouse of treats that can be found there! Cakes and bars, chocolate chips and nuts, all these and more, just waiting to be found for a quick nibble.

My biggest treat, though, turned out to be a treasure – standing just outside the pantry door. It happened in a dream. Something had been bothering me. Wine was becoming too large a presence in my life. I was distressed about it. What was I to do?

One night my father appeared in my dreams. Standing just outside the pantry door with his outstretched arms barring the entrance, he said to me, "Don't enter here!"

As I woke, the dream, like my dad, stood vivid in my mind. Pondering, I recalled a story my dad had told me many years ago: "You know, my doctor recommended that I have a glass of red wine each day because of my heart issues. I did this for quite some time. I would keep a bottle of wine on a shelf in the pantry. Then one day I realized that I was liking that wine a little too much. After that I stopped storing wine in the pantry."

The message in the dream was clear. It took me some time and some procrastination and more troubling thoughts, but one day I too stopped storing wine in the pantry.

Fragile Gifts

By Mark Bratlie

A dream may deliver an insight
    that helps us to learn and to grow,
Or it can be a reminder
    of something we already know.
A dream may arrive with abruptness,
    causing perceptions to shift,
Or it may glide through night's stillness
    to give sagging spirits a lift.
Sometimes a dream is quite fragile,
    a gift to be handled with care,
So if you value its sweetness,
    protect it from morning's sharp glare.
A dream may serve as a warning
    of mistakes about to be made,
So please take heed of the message
    before the day's light starts to fade.
Dreams can inform our life's journey,
    suggesting a path we might take.
Be sure you start down that pathway

when from the dream you awake.
Sometimes a dream is quite fragile,
a gift to be handled with care,
So if you value its sweetness,
protect it from morning's sharp glare.

Heeding the Call

I consider myself to be in training. No, not for the marathon, although I did do the 5k twice before I decided that I was not cut out to be a runner. Instead, I'm in training for being called into action. Or as my friend Linda says, paying attention to a "nudge from God". I've had a number of them happen, but this one stands out.

My colleague Mary Lou and I were standing by the kitchen table at work — it was 4:30 in the afternoon, and she was spooning down a yogurt while I was finger-picking a green salad. "Oh," she said with a sorrowful look, "Margie isn't doing very well at all. I don't think she has much longer." Margie was a mutual friend of ours and of our parents, and our history spread over many decades and multiple locations.

As I got into my car for the ride home, I thought, "I've just got to see her one more time!" I did have other obligations that evening, and once or twice on the way to visit Margie, I thought about turning back, but something kept me on my path.

Margie's gifts of friendship to me and to my parents over the years were many — brunches at her country place, her wonderful sour cream cookies still warm from the oven, and fish from her husband Jim's fishing trips – in exchange for bread baked by my mom.

So, when I walked into the nursing home that night, I rang the bell to summon the receptionist and said, "I'm here to see Margie Crowe."

She looked at me oddly and her eyes blinked. She paused, started to speak, and then paused again before saying, "Oh, Margie just passed away – just now passed away – it can't even have been a half hour." Startled by this news, I leaned against the counter. "Oh, no! She was such an incredibly sweet spirit!"

I paused and nothing further came from my mouth. "The family is still down in her room," the receptionist said, nodding her head toward the hallway.

I lingered and she said, "They're just starting to take some of her things out."

"What about her husband Jim?" I questioned.

"He's down there too."

I stood there, hesitating, and didn't move. I wondered about seeing Jim at this very tender moment. Would I know what to say? Perhaps I looked perplexed, so she said to me, "That's probably where the family is gathering."

What could I possibly do? What could I offer her family members? I lingered still, and then unsure of myself, I left.

Later that evening, in an attempt to clear my mind, I walked the park. Thoughts of Margie came to mind: how she'd healed my dad of severe back pain, how she'd prayed spontaneously for healing for me, and how she'd appeared so many times as a breath of spirit, a wing of prayer, or a tender touch. Margie didn't hesitate to step in when she saw a need to bring encouragement or comfort.

And then a different memory came to me – the people who had appeared unexpectedly at my own side, in my mom's hospital room, right after she had died. Less than two minutes after her passing, the phone on the stand next to my dear mother's body began ringing and ringing. I recalled my enormous reluctance to pick it up – and then on the fifth ring, hearing my friend Mary Ann's voice, I said,

"Mom just died." She replied, "I'll be right over," and so she was. Together we washed my mom's body.

Then there came a knock on the door, and my friend Burley entered; he'd heard in church that Mom was near death, and so he appeared. Then came Pastor Rich, with a word of comfort. Then came another friend, Linda. These were the blessed ones – the people who were called to be present. The people who had heard *"For a time such as this"* and had heeded the call.

Later I remembered where I'd first heard the phrase "*For a time such as this.*" It was from the Bible story of Esther who was called to intervene in a death threat to her Jewish people. She had resisted, but then was pressed by another: "Who knows whether, for a time such as this, you've been called to the kingdom?"

Now, when I consider that inner compulsion to drive to see Margie and then the step I took *away* from heeding the call, I feel differently. Now when I wonder if I should step forward or step away, I recall those words — "*For a time such as this"* — as a touchstone. And I remember Margie. Then I move forward.

Dis-Remembering Grudges

One of the most amusing tales I ever heard about recalling grudges or wrongs was told about Clara Barton, the founder of the American Red Cross. A friend reminded her of a cruel incident that had happened a few years past, but Barton couldn't seem to recall it.

"Don't you remember how awful that was?" the person asked.

"No," Barton answered calmly. "I distinctly remember forgetting that." Apparently, she didn't or she wouldn't allow the memory to seep into her consciousness.

And Nelson Mandela also had an opinion about the cost of resenting or bearing a grudge against another. He said, "Resentment is like drinking poison and then hoping it will kill your enemies."

Compared to Barton, and clearly Mandela, the wrongs in my life pale. But I've had my share of traumatic situations that have put me on the path to ugly emotions — emotions that could easily capture and hold me hostage. And big or small, they have to be worked through and released. If not, I suffer the consequences: preoccupation, loss of energy and vitality, and wasted time. Not to mention, possibly, illness.

How my wrongs have been resolved has varied — and that might be the lesson. We all have our ways, and there's no one way. They all take work and time. But sometimes there's a surprise at the end.

One such incident remains distinct in my memory.

My friend Jerome lived with me for half a year while he was transitioning from one locale to another. He was a dear soul — amusing, funny, creative — and ready to live a bit off of another's largesse if he could. Over the course of his stay, the good times piled up, but so too did the times when I wondered if I was being taken advantage of. In the end, instead of a planned departure, he left suddenly, leaving me with a small pile of bills for long-distance phone calls, his share of rent, and so on. Oh, I was mad, and my resentment began to build.

In retrospect, it all seems so silly now. What was $300-400 dollars? But of course, at the time it was a lot of money, and I didn't have the extra. I was angry and couldn't figure out how to deal with it. I knew the money was gone. Trying to retrieve it would be futile. Living near Loring Park, I headed outdoors to ventilate my emotions. It was during this walk – my third time stomping around the park – while I was silently cussing and cursing, when it suddenly came to me. What would happen if I could wish the very best for Jerome? Then it came to me like a bright light! As I'd realized long ago, if I could wish the very best for him, why, that in fact would bring the very best back to me.

Here is another incident.

I was trying to juggle the roles of being a caregiver for my mom and dad with being an advocate and steady sister to my brother David, who was fully disabled due to multiple sclerosis. Little by little my anger at my sister Shirley for not being here or doing more to help began eating at me. I also had a pressing full-time job, and I was having trouble keeping up. Even though my brother lived in a group home, my work with him was exhausting emotionally. His MS had affected him not only physically but also cognitively. While he remained extremely intelligent, sharp, and witty, his social skills and awareness of personal boundaries were so out-of-whack that it was difficult both for my parents and myself. Because of his behavior, David was moved from group home to group home.

The endless nature of my advocacy work on his behalf with the county social worker, comprehensive meetings with his group-home-care team, unexpected hospital stays for my parents and my brother, calls while I was at work to handle sudden situations, and the miles back and forth to do all this caring began to build up over a couple years time.

In many ways it was unrealistic for me to expect more from my sister Shirley. She lived 900 miles away. She had never been close to our younger brother, and she was enormously embarrassed and disturbed by his boundaryless nature. I understood that — I was too, but I saw up close how his behavior was a result of his illness, not his intentions or his true nature. A disease affecting the brain can make a person do inappropriate things.

These bad feelings against my sister Shirley did me no good, but I couldn't seem to escape them. That's the way with grudges. They invade your space. They wiggle in and take up residence in your mind. The question becomes whether or not you want them to stay.

As much as I stewed over the lack of my sister's support, I also kept up some key daily habits: meditation or devotional time, consistent exercise, and spending time each morning noting the happy things that had occurred the day before. My morning recollections of good things — or "thank yous" as I called them — were often very simple. It might be hearing the song of a cardinal while on a walk or remembering a gale of laughter at a friend's story. These delights formed an odd juxtaposition next to my grudges. How long could I keep this emotional seesaw going? Did I want to?

During meditation time one morning, I found myself aware of my web of frustration again. Was it misplaced anger? Was the source of my anger not really my sister but instead anger at the fate of my brother's life?

Meditation plays a trick sometimes. Once again, I caught myself stewing and pulled myself back to deep breathing. Suddenly there appeared in my mind's eye an image of Shirley and her husband Al, enveloped in a golden haze, high in the sky. My anger vanished. In an instant. And it never returned.

How could that be? How could my heart be healed, and the anger vanquished? It's the opposite of what happens when a grudge burrows into your spirit. This was more like a butterfly breaking out of a cocoon.

It came as a result of hard work, meditation, and a big splurge of grace.

The book, *Cherokee Feast of Days, Daily Meditations*, by Joyce Sequichie Hifler, often brings quiet insights my way. Here is one that suggests a more peaceful way to live:

"Someday, we will know how to take living in stride, to sidestep a great many things and completely ignore that many more. Sometime, we will learn to pay less attention to the imagined and stop fussing about things we had nothing to do with in the past —and cannot change significantly in the future. One day, like the elderly Cherokee, we can say, 'So long a time since I see you…I don't care anymore.' Soon, we will rid ourselves of things we saved for no good reason and have room for what we really want. As soon as possible, we will worry less about trouble … knowing some people need it for their security. Very soon, we will sit together in the sun a whole day and just be happy that we can sit together in the sun all day and just be happy."

This is the way I now choose to live in my world—"Very soon, we will sit together in the sun a whole day and just be happy."

CHAPTER 4

Loving and Letting Go

A Certain Kind of Death

Dad and I talked about suicide every now and then – probably because every now and then it happened to someone we knew. A neighbor. A community person. A friend.

During these conversations, we talked about the particulars surrounding these deaths. Then my response: "Well, clearly the person wasn't well or in their right mind!" Dad would nod, his eyes gazing far away, and with a face full of compassion, he'd say, "But oh, it's tough for the family that's left."

Those conversations about suicide and my dad's kind face have remained crystal clear in my mind. Somehow they've given me a visual reminder of how to face any loss, any kind of change – with courage. They remind me to look ahead, to hold close what is precious, and then over time to let the sorrow pass through and away from me.

Is any death easy? Not if it's somebody you love. Sudden? Prolonged? Unexpected? So many different stories, but they all end the same way. With your world an echoing, empty place – a vacuum where there was once a living being. And now, with this shocking absence, and your ruined hopes, you have to make your way into the future. We all do.

Saving Grace

The phone call came from my brother-in-law Al, as I was walking with my 88-year-old mom from the pool area up to her apartment in her senior living community.

I couldn't find my cell phone in my bag and so it went to message. I thought it was just as well, because my first order of business since flying home from a visit to relatives in Portland, Oregon, was to stop and say hello to my mom. We often loved to go down to the pool area where she'd sit and enjoy the plants and cheer me on as I swam. "Oh, that looks like fun!" she'd exclaim, delighted to see me paddling about. After the flight, I knew that a swim in the pool would be a refreshing break.

My sister Shirley had been invited to join me in the visit to see our Aunt Alice and Cousin Lois in Oregon, but she was a disciplined quilter and a big sale on quilting supplies was being held that weekend. At first, I couldn't quite believe that she'd choose the quilt sale over the trip, but then it made sense to me, given her dedication to her craft and her love of a good deal.

Upstairs now in Mom's apartment, I checked my phone for a message. Al's voice, sounding very strained said, "Something's happened at home. I'm at the Chicago airport and catching another flight soon." That was it. No explanation.

My heart stopped for a moment. "Something's happened at home?" What could it be? My nieces? Had there been a car accident? Even though the girls, as I still called them, were grown, married, and living elsewhere, I thought they might have come to some harm.

I tried calling Al back, but there was no answer, just messaging. Quickly, I called my sister Shirley at their home in Colorado Springs – but no answer there either, just a rollover into voice mail. This was extremely odd because Shirley, being an early-to-bed person, was always home by this time.

It was then that I recalled my strange experience of waking up very early on the Sunday morning of my trip – crying, with a clenched stomach and Shirley on my mind. I had thought of calling her right then – but hesitated. It was 4:30 in the morning, and certainly I would wake both her and Al up. My anxiety continued through the day, and I tried calling, but no answer and I never tried again.

Now, moving out of earshot to Mom's bedroom phone, to not alarm her, I called my niece Karen who lived with her husband Abel, a couple of hours away from her parents, Al and Shirley.

"Haven't you talked with Al?" Karen cried out. "Mom died!" Then I heard a half-sob. "She may have committed suicide." Another sob.

A silence followed and then Karen said shakily, "Are you there?"

"Yes," I said, "I'm here at Mom's apartment. She can't hear us." I'd fallen to my knees as the terrible words sank into me.

"Karen, even if Shirley did commit suicide, she wouldn't have been in her right mind." This thought came immediately to me because it was what my dad and I had always said when we had discussed the concept of suicide in days gone by.

Oh, how I longed to comfort Karen, but she was inconsolable. Then I made a call to my niece Jill. I had to hear her voice, too, though it was impossible for us to offer enough comfort to each other.

Oddly enough, I couldn't bear to tell my mother that evening that her first-born, her Shirley, had died. Perhaps it was because this was the second death of her three children, her youngest and her oldest, in two years, and it followed just two months after the death of her dear husband of 59 years, Lynn.

Whatever the reason – probably shock too – I kept the news to myself that night. I told Mom I would see her in the morning. We did final good-night hugs and "I love yous" before I headed home.

The next morning, with my godmother Grace and cousin Gayle at my side, we sat together on my mom's sofa, and I told her that Shirley had passed away. I saw her lips tremble and her face crumple, and her eyes took on a new look as they began to see her changed world.

Turning to me she said, "Oh, I've lost David . . . I've lost Dad . . . and now Shirley!" She reached out and touched my knee and said, "Now Jeannie, you hang in there."

It was hard to fathom what had happened that early Sunday morning after my brother-in-law Al had left Shirley for his business trip out east. Their routine had been to call each other daily when one was away from the other, and Al did so on Sunday — but with no response. Because of Shirley's early-to-bed habit, he didn't try later that evening.

On Monday, still receiving no answer, Al became worried and asked their neighbor, Cala, to get the key from the garage and check the house. As Cala and her son opened the garage door to retrieve the key, the outcome was apparent. There was Shirley, slumped over in the car, the gas fumes in the garage overpowering.

Later, I asked Cala an odd question, given the circumstances. "Did you get a chance to say goodbye?" Her immediate response to me was a gift from the angels: "No, but she looked so peaceful," Cala said. These were the words that I would return to many times as a balm for my painful loss.

We'll never know in this lifetime the full story of what happened. There was no note and no immediate apparent reason for suicide. It could have been a bizarre accident.

The weekend of her death, Shirley had celebrated her 60th birthday and purchased special equipment for her quilting machine, plus a new file drawer for the place she worked part time as a dietitian. She had already planned for future activities, including an application to participate in an upcoming quilt show. She loved her two daughters and husband Al enormously, and a week after her death, a package with clothing tags saying, "*Made especially for you by Grandma Hassebrock,*" arrived in the mail. She'd ordered them for the sundress she was making for her new granddaughter, Aidan Lynn.

A friend of mine, a highly regarded behavioral therapist in whom I had great trust, said to me after I'd told her the story: "If a family had presented this to me, I would have called it an accident. She may have been so sleep-deprived that she just said, 'I'll start the car and rest a minute.' In those instances, there's no time to self-correct. She was futuristic in her plans, and those are the ones we don't worry about."

Nonetheless, Shirley had suffered not only from sleep deprivation but from bipolar disorder and depression for over 20 years. Though it might have been an accident, suicide was what we had to believe.

What I found especially hard were the questions from friends and neighbors: "What happened? She was so young. Did she have a heart attack?"

I just couldn't bring myself to say, "She committed suicide." I'd always thought it a poor way to describe the death of someone who suffered from mental illness or depression.

My friend Dy helped me through it when, on the very first day after I'd arrived home from Colorado Springs, she rang my doorbell and said that she'd learned how Shirley died. My sobs made my distress clear as I heatedly said, "Bad enough that she's gone so suddenly – but how it happened!" Sobbing, I went on to say, "It's not right or fair to say she committed suicide or took her own life. I say that she had a chemical imbalance or a brain attack."

Our family's saving grace was the bond with Shirley that we had built among us over a lifetime. Our hearts were meant to help each other heal.

Upon my return back home from the prayer and memorial services in Colorado, I found among the cards and envelopes one from a dear old friend, who'd included a token of sympathy from his daughter Alberta. She was a very young artist and had fashioned a simple white bird out of a fuzzy white cloth, and in the center were two hearts – one pink and one orange, with black stitches holding the hearts together. It became a literal touchstone – providing adornment for the notebook I was using to write my early morning thoughts, and an emblem of hearts yearning to heal together.

Each of us returned to our homes with hearts to heal. We kept in touch. Al told us about spotting a cat, which he'd never seen before, waiting and watching for him in an alleyway on his walk to church. The cat came up to him, moved around his leg, and walked with him as he took the Sunday morning walk to church without Shirley. It was a walk that they'd taken hundreds of times before. He believed that the cat was Shirley's spirit coming to comfort him. In his telling of that story, he comforted us.

My niece Karen's pregnancy weighed especially heavy on my mind. I couldn't imagine the turmoil and sadness that she must be facing. But one morning, just a couple of weeks after Shirley's death, I was surprised and lifted by the Bible passage I found: "*Among them will be the blind and the lame, expectant mothers and women in labor, a great throng will return. They will come with weeping; they will pray as I bring them back. I will lead them beside streams of water on a level path where they will not stumble . . .* " *(*Jeremiah 31:8, New International Version*).*

I wanted to face things head on, and so I began each day before going to work in a favorite chair, with the bird with the hearts stitched together as my touchstone and a notebook and Bible in my hand. Because it was so early in the morning, the tears and thoughts came easily – they weren't covered up by events and activities of the day.

One of the first days, readying my coffee in the kitchen, I heard a fluttering sound and looking about to locate the source, I found a long-ago taped clipping from a church bulletin falling on the floor: "*The Spirit of the Lord God is upon me, because the Lord has anointed me; the Lord has sent me to bring good news to the oppressed, to bind up the broken hearted . . . to comfort all who mourn;*

to provide those who mourn in Zion – to given them a garland instead of ashes, the oil of gladness instead of mourning, the mantle of praise instead of a faint spirit. They will be called oaks of righteousness, the planting of the Lord, to display the Lord's glory." (Isaiah 61: 1-4 and 8-11, New Revised Standard Version).

Perhaps a large key to our healing as a family were Karen's words: "Nobody is blaming anyone and nobody is denying anything."

I realized later that all these things – Al's cat story, Karen's words, and the fluttering Bible passage – are the things I come back to for comfort, when Shirley's death and all that surrounds it gets to be too tough to take in. They provide an oasis of calm and balm, and they allow me the space to remember Shirley with affection and joy.

No matter the cause of Shirley's death, I know that she's been welcomed by God and that she is at rest. And if she is at rest, I can be too.

Wide Open

By Jean Anderson

Driving in spring through the great wide open,
past farmland ditches swollen with water,
with geese streaking the early morning sky.
Heading north, I think,
Oh, how I love the country.
Suddenly a news flash on the radio:
"Jill Carroll, freelance journalist held hostage in Iraq,
has been freed. She is alive."
The news brings tears to my eyes –
Then more on a second hearing. Why?
At first I'm not sure.
Later, I'm finished with my work
in the small towns of North Dakota,
and suddenly my sister Shirley comes to mind.
I cry again at her early unexpected death.
I miss her so, feel lonesome for her, think about her often.
Something is bringing Shirley so close and tender.
I wonder why today, especially, am I feeling this?
Perhaps it's the wide expanse of countryside

and travel time that lets thoughts and tears fill and flow.
There is no busy-ness crowding my mind –
Just me and the melting earth and the gray sky
And the solo road I'm traveling on.
Tonight though, this comes to me:
Jill, the freelance journalist, has been
found alive. If only Shirley was.

A Falling Leaf
By Mark Bratlie

Today a leaf came down to greet me,
falling gently on a breeze
With intentions to remind me
of the things I must release.
Nature teaches of life's cycles,
when to cling and when to fall.
There is a time for every season
and solace if we hear the call.
But letting go is not so easy,
we may need more than just a breeze.
Graceful falling takes some practice
and a lesson from the trees.
This human mind is often yearning
for some past or future day,
But opening to present stillness
allows a more fulfilling way.
We cannot control our seasons –
grasping only brings more grief.
Let us settle in the moment
like the falling of a leaf.

CHAPTER 5

New Life With Light

Jim's Life and Death

The good news was that I had a new job as Director of Development at Hospice of the Red River Valley. As I chatted with people – from the man fixing my doorbell to the owner of the local candy store – and told them of my new work, I was struck by how many people had hospice stories to tell. Stories of hope, grace, and life.

Then during my first few weeks of work, while I was visiting the Detroit Lakes Hospice office, the director pointed out a picture of two men and their snowmobiles. She told me that one of the men, Jim, had been a hospice patient. The other man in the picture was his brother Bob. You can imagine how incredulous I was when she told me the picture had been taken the day before Jim died.

A few days later I talked to Jim's loving companion Patty. She told me that Jim was a man who enjoyed skiing, snowmobiling, and working with his hands. He had owned his own car repair shop and loved working as a mechanic. One day he felt a sharp pain under his ribs. Two weeks later he was diagnosed with advanced colon cancer. It had spread to his liver. The doctor gave him two months to two years to live.

Jim lived for only two months; yet Jim lived those two months in the same way that he had lived for 50 years – he packed in as much living as possible. With Patty's help he managed to travel to see his childhood friends in Grand Rapids, visit his dad's grave, buy his daughter a laptop, and see his mom in Duluth. After all this, Jim was too weak to travel back home, so he and Patty stayed an extra night at his mom's.

When they finally reached home, Jim told Patty that he wanted to "go" – he was getting tired. Then his brother Bob arrived from South Dakota. Although Jim was moving through the dying stages, he rallied when he saw his brother. Two days after Bob arrived, Jim was taking his pills and yogurt when he said to Patty: "I think I'm going to go for a snowmobile ride today – we've got two sleds out there, and Bob and I have been talking about snowmobiling for days."

Patty couldn't believe what she'd heard. She was terrified that Jim couldn't do it, and that if he did do it, he wouldn't return alive. She pressed him: "*Why* do you want to do this?" Jim's response was short and to the point: "I never went on a snowmobile ride with my brother and I want to do it before I die."

She thought: "If he's going to try to do this, I'm not going to help him. He'll be tired before he gets to the door." So she watched as Jim, from his hospice bed, struggled to put on his boots, liners, leathers, and helmet. "Oh, he worked so hard to get dressed – it took him nearly an hour!" she said. Still Patty didn't want to let him go. She confided to me: "At this point, I was protecting *myself.*" But as she hemmed and hawed and tried to dissuade him, Jim leaned towards her and said, "Why don't you quit being so overprotective and just kiss me?"

Jim's brother Bob, who was as terrified as Patty about losing Jim, started the snowmobiles and promised Patty, "We won't go fast and we won't jump anything." Fifteen minutes later they returned from the ride. Jim took off his helmet, put out his hand to shake Bob's, and said, "That was a good ride!"

For the rest of the day Jim had the biggest smile on his face. Patty remarked, "He was beaming, just beaming."

Then around supper time, as he rested, still in his leathers, Jim started his journey towards death. He began talking to people that only he could see. As he drifted in and out, his voice suddenly became clear and he said, "Yes, I know – I'm coming. I'm just not in a hurry right now." Patty believes he must have been talking either to the angels or to his dad.

Early the next afternoon, with hospice nurse Betty, his children, his brother Bob, and Patty in the room, Jim died. He had lived fully up until the moment of his death.

The founder of the first modern hospice, English physician Dame Cicely Saunders, spoke about the reason for hospice, saying: "*We will do all we can, not only to help you die peacefully, but also to help you live until you die.*"

And that's how hospice helped Jim live until he died. Patty told me, "There was such peace in that room. Jim did it the way he wanted, and without hospice he couldn't have. He would have been in the hospital, and he would have been connected to tubes."

Later she remarked to me, "You can die with dignity and grace and happiness ... you can. I know because I saw Jim do it."

Light On His Feet

My favorite — and only — brother David died at age 50 from complications of multiple sclerosis. He slipped away in his sleep while I snoozed at his bedside in a cushy big recliner.

Earlier the previous afternoon, David had been transferred to the palliative care unit by ambulance. He came to while the paramedics were tending to him, and he remained alert for a couple of hours afterwards.

Now I stood with Nicolle, a social worker for Hospice of the Red River Valley, at his new bedside to let David know that the end of his life was near. How had this happened so suddenly? Just two days earlier David had been bugging me about getting him pots and pans for his long-hoped-for return to independent living.

Nicolle introduced herself to him by saying, "I'm Nicolle and I'm here to tell you a bit about what the doctors are thinking. I work with your sister Jean at Hospice of the Red River Valley." Upon hearing this, David, in a classic Three Stooges maneuver — a mock horror shrug with his shoulders and face, plus a hocus-pocus move with his hands to ward off evil – absorbed the news. Then in a voice strained by his six days of wearing an oxygen mask, David asked Nicolle, "Are you getting combat pay for this?" We all laughed.

Later, in a quiet room, Nicolle said to me, "My, he is light on his feet. He doesn't take himself too seriously, does he?" I thought it was an odd comment, since David was reclining in his bed when we spoke with him. And though God had graced David with his MS wish — the ability to always walk – David's walk could be more of a lurch and a lumber than a dancer's light tread.

Then it came to me later in a flash – Nicolle's words about David were indeed the perfect description of the gift God had given David – being light on his feet.

Despite the myriad of very drastic, even cataclysmic changes that came into David's life because of the disease of MS, he possessed an uncanny ability to land on his feet – with a mind and a heart that were still quick, warm, and witty.

God's gift to my brother David turned out to be David's gift to our family and to many who knew him.

Because of this, I will now always remember him as David Lawrence *Light-on-His-Feet* Anderson.

My Brother's Last Gift

"This might be an odd question, but do you wish he would have left it all to you?" My friend Camille posed this challenge to me over the phone one night as we were talking about my brother David's death and resulting estate.

"Estate" seems an odd word since David had lived 25 years of his short life as a poor man. On the flight home from his international law internship in Denmark, he started having double-vision, the first symptom he would experience of the ugly disease of multiple sclerosis. So, my brother never had the kind of income one might associate with a future career as an attorney. Instead, a $504 Social Security disability check came to him each month.

When he died unexpectedly at age 50, however, he suddenly became "rich". A life insurance policy he had purchased as a young law student paid out $70,000 to his estate. His estate in this case meant me, plus three charitable organizations: Comstock Lutheran Church and Crystal Cathedral (the spiritual homes of his youth and short life) and his alma mater, Gustavus Adolphus College.

I didn't know who would inherit his estate until two friends and I were clearing out his room after he died. I found among his files one marked *Will.* I flinched at seeing the cold reality of his death. I opened the file and found a plain business envelope and a yellow sheet of paper filled with David's crab-like handwriting and the beginning words, "*I, David Lawrence Anderson, being of sound mind and body (sort of)* . . . ." I burst out laughing and knew in that instant that David's legacy gifts to me were clearly his humor and his steadfast spirit of dogged hope.

But my friend's question – "Did you want it all?" – lingered. At first, I thought, "Yes, I did want more." Given a chance, I'm always able to think of a few wonderful things to do or buy if I just had more money.

But in actuality, the answer to my friend was "No." I didn't want all my brother's money. What I really wanted, of course, was to have my brother back, but that wasn't about to happen. And before David's unexpected death, what we had all wanted was to have some of his life insurance released early so that he could have lived an easier life, but that never came to pass.

The extra time I wanted with my brother did come to me in an unexpected way. During the months after David died, some of the most cherished moments my family and I had were thinking about, preparing for, and disbursing the gifts David left to his favorite charities.

In November, on the anniversary of his death, my family and friends from Comstock Lutheran Church ate muffins, David's favorite food. We put a birthday candle in each one and sang "Happy Birthday" to celebrate the first year of his new life in heaven. Then we honored his generous spirit by handing a check over for the benefit of the church's work. We shed a few tears, but we also had some good laughs.

The following year, my niece Karen and I traveled to California to deliver some of David's legacy to the Crystal Cathedral. And in one final tribute to my brother, an endowed scholarship has been established at Gustavus Adolphus College in David's name. For years to come, a student will benefit from his generosity.

One of the unusual outcomes of all of David's giving has been its quiet impact on my own thinking. Now I realize deep in my core the sweet satisfaction that comes when you get to be the transporter to the community of someone else's generosity.

Because I miss my brother dearly, I've discovered that a great goodness and grace exists in bringing him to life via his gifts to others. Not only do we get to pass on David's generosity, but we can also recall and pass on his humor and optimism.

Since my brother's death, I look at estate gifts in a whole new way. They are a way to leave another kind of legacy. This one is to your family – the legacy of a generous spirit.

"But I Need Your Help"

The phone call from the doctor came with a message that made my stomach sink, and tears started to flow after I heard his words: "I was really surprised to find this, but you have Hepatitis C."

Hepatitis C? What? "What is that?" I asked. Though he'd mentioned the disease at my last appointment with him, we'd brushed it aside as another possibility to explore the symptoms I'd had for well over a year.

"It's a disease of the liver, caused by a virus, and inflammation occurs. It can be very serious and, in some instances, lead to death – if treatments aren't discovered and successful in controlling or curing the disease. It explains the episodes you are having. I'm going to refer you to a gastroenterologist who specializes in liver diseases, and then you can decide what you want to do next."

I remembered the last visit to the doctor's office – it seemed that I had been a regular at the clinic over the past year. "General malaise" is how the details of the doctor's notes read. I had to look the word up – malaise – was that what I was suffering from? It sounded so simple and harmless, but oh, how general malaise had changed my life.

One evening over supper with friends I said, "I'm really concerned. Something just isn't right with me. I keep having these spells when I feel really, really sick. It's like a cloud swoops in out of the blue and settles over me, and it feels like a poison. It's changing how I live — I'm taking sick leave and I'm missing out on fun events." Breaking into sobs I said, "I don't know what it is, but something is wrong. I know what health is and this isn't it."

My friends were alarmed. Sue said, "You've got to get to the bottom of this."

That conversation gave me the courage to continue to press my doctor for more answers. Over the course of a number of visits, we had tried many things, and I was beginning to feel like a repeat customer with continuing complaints and no reprieve in sight. Whenever I had a spell, I would call and make the appointment, although of course, whenever I landed at his office, my body and my spirits would seem to be working just fine.

Finally, after the last simple idea by the doctor – more upper body exercise to address stress issues – failed, I'd had it. In great frustration, probably matched by his own, I cried out, "Look! We need to get to the bottom of this." He was as frustrated as I was, and he said with a shrug of his shoulders, "Well, you don't have any of the risk factors, but there's a test now for Hepatitis C, so we'll try that."

Sure enough, that test did the trick, and found the source of my symptoms.

And so the long haul began. The initial treatments were experimental – the FDA had recently approved a trial procedure for Hepatitis C. I was one of a group of people who were randomly assigned a mix of pills and injections, all done on a daily basis for a six-month period of time. Some were placebos and some were real.

Oh, what a ray of hope these treatments were! But the treatments proved to be almost as difficult to bear as the illness they were aiming to cure. There were a number of side effects. Though I escaped the dreaded debilitating depression, I had great body ache, fatigue, and more general malaise that became the order of the day. I often found myself soaking in the bathtub in the middle of the night in order to help ease the aching that wracked my body.

However, the initial trial procedures went well enough, and the FDA lifted its cover on the trial in the midst of my second stretch of treatments. Being ill is like being in a strange land. Normal life – whatever that is – drifts away, and in its place are doctor appointments, treatment regimes, and their after-effects. In my case it also meant a reduced work schedule and a seriously curtailed social calendar.

Your spirits are the hardest thing to keep up when you're ill over a period of time. During the past couple of years there had been many events and joys of life that I had had to give up because I'd been sick or hadn't had the energy to participate. My family and friends had been terrifically supportive, and yet I'd spent a lot of time at home alone.

I was scheduled to travel to see my best friend's son, Isaac, perform in his final high school band concert. This would require driving about five hours to reach

Stillwater, the small town where they lived. I'd been eagerly anticipating this musical event for several months.

On the afternoon I was to leave for my weekend in Stillwater, I was lying on the couch in my living room. Though I hadn't felt well for a few days, I thought that, like some other occasions, the symptoms would lift and I could go. Time passed and I kept thinking, "I bet in an hour I'll feel better." And then when that didn't work, I said to myself, "I bet if I have a cup of tea and wait another hour, I'll feel better." And then, "I bet if I just lie down again, I'll feel better. I can just start on the trip a little later – maybe tomorrow morning." The hours passed but the illness didn't. I thought, "Well, if I just get up and start packing, I'm sure I'll be able to . . ."

But finally I realized that despite all my hope, longing, and determination, the idea of getting up and packing my suitcase was beyond me. I couldn't imagine doing that, let alone driving for five hours. It was out of the question. It was all too much for me. I was truly ill. Once again, I had to admit it.

In a voice laced with steel, to guard against the enormous disappointment I was feeling, I called and reported this to my friend Camille. We were both deeply discouraged. The call was short. When I hung up, I broke into sobs of despair and loneliness. Was I ever going to get well? Was I ever going to be able to do normal things again? Was this to be my future? Suddenly, as though a person sitting right next to me was speaking, a voice – clear and strong as a gong – said: "I'm healing you now, but I need your help."

"I'm healing you now, but I need your help." Was I hearing things? Well, yes, I was, but the voice rang out so strong that the air cleared around me, and the words set off a vibration within me.

The sentence I heard was clear and direct: "*I'm healing you now, but I need your help.*" There was no mistaking it. It was a blessing and a command. I listened intently.

I lay back down on the couch, contemplating the strange comfort that I had been given. I fell fast into a deep sleep. When I woke up, I realized that my life had changed. Oh, the symptoms didn't disappear, and the regimen of treatment that I was on for round two didn't work. I had to start anew with more potent drugs, and it took another year and a half before my doctor said the word “Cured”. But in the meantime, I was revived in a way that I had never expected.

The words I heard that day gave me the encouragement and the knowledge to keep on the path. They sustained me at a time when I felt bereft of hope. Their blessing has been one that has remained with me to this day because they gave me a window into the whole of healing. I could trust that God was working to heal me, and I could recognize that I had a major part to play in it. My part was to rest.

CHAPTER 6

Family Gifts

Try Shaping Your Character

"It was created for children, but we found that it was well-suited for the monks here at the monastery too." These were the words spoken by our guide at the Hindu monastery as he held up the loosely bound volume, *A Character Building Workbook.*

Good for children and for monks? What about for those of us in between? And what exactly is character building anyway? I was intrigued enough to purchase a copy and bring it home from our Kauai travels.

"Character" – a word that's easily recognizable, but not easy to define! Looking at the index in the booklet, I found 64 words, listed in alphabetical order, that suddenly made the word "character" real: "Abstemious, Accepting, Affectionate, Appreciative, Attentive, Available, Calm, Cautious, Chaste, Clean, Compassionate, Consistent, Content, Courageous, Courteous, Creative, Curious, Decisive, Diligent, Discerning, Discreet, Enduring, Flexible, Forging, Frugal, Generous, Gentle, Grateful, Honest, Hospitable, Humble, Having Initiative, Having Integrity, Joyful, Loyal, Non-Hurtful, Non-Stealing,

Obedient, Open-Minded, Optimistic, Orderly, Patient, Persuasive, Philomathic, Playful, Punctual, Reliable, Remorseful, Respectful, Self-Confident, Self-Controlled, Self-Disciplined, Selfless, Sensitive, Sharing, Sincere, Spiritual, Steadfast, Tactful, Thorough, Thrifty, Tolerant, Truthful," and lastly, "Wise." All qualities that help shape a person's moral or mental life.

At first I thought, "Aren't I a little old to begin character building?" But then I thought of our former president, Donald J. Trump, a 77- year-old, who I sorely wish would do some self-reflection and character building. I decided I'd start.

I sat with those words – those qualities — for quite some time, pondering which I could lay claim to and which were in need of strengthening. And then in a quick motion, I snapped up a pen and started making stars by the ones that struck me as needing attention: Abstemious, Content, Frugal, Joyful, Non-Hurtful, Self-Controlled, Self-Disciplined, Thrifty.

I read the full list of character building qualities to a friend, and then I shared the ones I'd starred. My friend said, "I never would have chosen those words for you! It's so intriguing to see what a person comes up with for themselves, as compared to what others might think."

Now, six months later, I find myself choosing different qualities that need bolstering. For that I'm grateful. It turns out that changes in life circumstances bring different qualities to the forefront – both qualities that shine and qualities that need attention.

One character trait lesson I learned early in life was vivid in its visual nature: Generous. Posted on a pillar in the seed-cleaning plant that my dad operated on our farm was this message meant for anyone to see, but especially the young men he employed. The note, written in my dad's own hand, faced the person who was filling the seed bags: "Give and it will be given to you; good measure, pressed down, shaken together, running over . . . For the measure you give will be the measure you get back." This Biblical quote from Luke 6:38 provided clear instruction on the proper way to fill the seed bags for the customers. And added a quiet life lesson as well.

Another trait learned early was Hospitality. Social events in our home during my growing-up years were common. Rugs were rolled up, tables and chairs moved to make room for square dancing, plus Mom and Dad hosted whist card parties, come-as-you-are parties, birthday and anniversary parties, picnics, and gatherings for no good reason—other than to get together. Mom once told me as she was leaving for an event at a neighbor's home, "There wouldn't be a party if no one came." People came.

Of course, that was in the last century! Since then, my parents have died and the pandemic struck. Hospitality has gone by the wayside. The pandemic surely put a damper on my own hospitality. Perhaps it's time to begin again.

Which leads me to think that different eras do call for different traits. What traits did the pandemic need most? How about: Compassionate, Available, Non-Hurtful, Patient, Flexible, Selfless, Spiritual, and Wise?

Sometimes, in my bleaker moments, I wonder what happened to admiring strong character traits. It seems the world now most often celebrates those that glitter and glow. Or those that speak the loudest. It's better to probe for what is good.

I rather like the way we sometimes speak about a person — "Oh, he's quite a character!" It means they have some outstanding characteristic: humor, or artistry, or something unusual that makes them stand out. Oftentimes, it's an eccentric trait, or something in excess. But it does make them memorable.

Historian Warren Susman in his book, *Culture as History*, says the use of the phrase "good character" peaked in the 19th century. It was promoted as an "essential component of one's identity." Now it sounds a bit old-fashioned. But we might do well to acknowledge that it still has life—and make it a more central part of our own lives.

A Story About Faith, Healing, and My Dad

My dad was a farmer and a seedsman living in Holy Cross Township in Minnesota. He'd lived for 80 of his 89 years on the same land and in the same house in which he was born. It was the beauty of all the seasons of farm work that helped to make him such a grounded man of great faith. Humble and humorous, with a light heart and an optimistic nature, he told me this story of healing. It has made me a believer in the power and miracle of prayer.

Margie Crowe, our neighbor in this story, grew up in the South and had a strong Christian faith. She and her husband James co-owned Bergstrom and Crowe, a furniture store in downtown Fargo. She was a charming woman of means, with a lake home, a ranch in Texas, a condo in Fargo, and a farm home on the Red River.

My mom Ruth Ann and my dad Lynn grew close with Margie and Jim over the last decades of their lives, since they were farm neighbors living just a few miles apart.

This story was told by my dad.

~ ~ ~

"I remember it just as though it was yesterday," Dad said when I asked him about the amazing healing. Nearly 25 years had passed since then, but the minutes when he and Margie, his neighbor from down the road, were together in our farmyard were still vivid to him. He went on:

"The pain I was having was so bad that I thought I was maybe having a heart attack. And so your momma and I went to the clinic, but they couldn't find anything wrong with me. But, oh man, I was in such pain! It was as if someone was pushing a hot iron rod into my chest, and I felt like a piece of cold iron against it. The pain in my shoulder was almost unbearable. Twice I went to the emergency room that week, and finally they decided it was muscle fibrillation, which felt like 'spine out of whack' to me."

"I suppose the problem started when I was mowing grass in the ditch in the north driveway. The ditch was pretty steep – and the mower and I were tilted a lot — so I think I got what is incorrectly called a slipped disc. I don't know what the medical people would call it. This happened about two weeks before the healing."

"I was up many nights as I sat in a chair and tried to sleep. I had extreme pain in my shoulder day and night. The pillows were piled all around me, and I said to myself in disbelief, 'Lynn, this can't be possible.' And yes, I was praying, but I wasn't getting anywhere."

"Then on June 18, 1979, the 110th Bernhardson family reunion was held at our farm. I asked my brother Mel to take over leading the festivities because I was still having such pain. I had to keep my arm over my shoulder in order to lessen the agony. Somehow, I got through that reunion."

"The following morning Mom and the ladies held Bible class and a prayer meeting at Margie's. When Momma came home, she reported that the five or six ladies had all prayed for me."

"The next thing I heard was the sound of gravel crunching, and here comes Margie driving into the yard. I remember walking down the sidewalk to meet her, and her first words to me were, 'Are you having health or physical problems?' 'Yes!' I told her, 'I've got this pain in my back and shoulder and I can't shake it.'"

"Margie said, 'Yes, I heard you're in great pain. Let's go sit in the car.' As we walked towards the car she said, 'You know what James has to say about this don't you?'" I thought for a moment that she meant her husband James, but then I realized she meant the Biblical James, son of Zebedee."

"Margie went on speaking James' words: 'Is any one of you sick? He should call the elders of the church to pray over him and anoint him with oil in the name of the Lord. And the prayer offered up in faith will make the sick person well; the Lord will raise him up. If he has sinned, he will be forgiven. Therefore, confess your sins to each other and pray for each other so that you may be healed. The prayer of a righteous man is powerful and effective."

"Although I couldn't call right to mind any special sins of unbelief or sins of omission or commission that I had to confess, Margie looked straight into my eyes, touched my shoulder, and said with conviction, 'You're prepared and I'm an elder in the Presbyterian Church. Let's pray about it.'"

"Margie laid her hand on my shoulder and prayed for me and asked God to remove the pain. The pain vanished. It was instantaneous. In fact, it was faster than that. So, this old Lutheran said, 'Hallelujah — Praise the Lord!' And within a few minutes, feeling such relief, I headed for the seed plant to work for the rest of the day. The pain was gone. Gone!"

"Later I went to a chiropractor for a remaining ache. My left shoulder was drawn back and forth, and it took three or four months to recover fully, but those first weeks of horrendous pain were gone with Margie's touch and prayer, and it didn't bother me one speck after that. Oh, my arm would get tired after a while, but it never hurt that same way again."

"It was a total spiritual experience. So, I'm a believer. I try to compliment Margie whenever I can, to tell her how thankful I was for her intercession. There wasn't any hocus-pocus, and it wasn't even Margie herself. She was just a tool. Ever since then, I've thought that we should do a little more of the laying on of hands to help each other."

~ ~ ~

My dad's words have stayed with me through the years. He lived his faith daily in word and deed. And I believe it was his openness towards the miraculous and creation that allowed him the gift of healing.

A Surprise Inheritance

As a redhead with a flair for color, my Aunt Lois was a quilter by avocation. One of my favorite photos shows her standing in the farmyard where I grew up, arms aloft and spread wide in the sunlight, holding a lavender quilt that she'd made. Both her hair and the quilt blow in the breeze, and a broad smile spreads across her face.

Aunt Lois and her family lived in Michigan, but they spent many summers at my family's farm in Minnesota. George, her husband, would take education classes at NDSU, a land-grant university in Fargo, the town where she and my mom grew up. When we greeted them at the train station each summer as they arrived, the night train's incoming whistle seemed to alert us to an especially happy summer ahead.

We had to shift our sleeping arrangements in the big farmhouse to accommodate four more people. My own bedroom became the bedroom for my Aunt Lois and Uncle George. A plywood board was placed under the mattress to make the bed more comfortable for my aunt, who had back problems. I loved my new summer bedroom — the big sleeping porch that was surrounded with windows and screens on three sides. Looking out, I was at tree-leaf level, and the night sky stretched wide above me. Our spare bedroom became the sleeping spot for my cousins.

My cousins Richard and Paul, along with my sister Shirley and brother David, were my summer-time playmates. The great openness of the farm as well as the fields, picnics, and rides at the county fair were things we all loved. Jumping over stacked seed sacks in the barn proved great fun, although such hurdling also landed Richard in the local emergency room with two broken wrists. Yes, we had adventures.

A librarian by profession, Aunt Lois was fond of the printed word and had wide-ranging tastes. I liked taking book suggestions from her, and one of my favorites was *Undaunted Courage*, the story of the Lewis and Clark journey through the West. She once remarked to me that after she could list having worked at the Harvard Law Library on her resume, she never again worried about being hired.

Lois had the travel bug. Her last journey in life was a trip to Scotland with a group from her church. On their first night in Edinburgh, they went out for dinner and a photo was taken. There was Aunt Lois at the end of the long wooden table with a big smile and her hand held high waving hello. But that hello-wave turned out to be a good-bye wave as well.

Late that night, Lois got up from her bed and collapsed because of a stroke. Luckily, she had a roommate who got others' attention, and Lois was rushed to the hospital.

In a big circular ward in the Royal Edinburgh Hospital, she lived for 11 days, long enough for both of her sons to cross the ocean to spend time with her. They were fortunate enough to feel the squeeze of her hand and to say their good-byes.

As she lingered between life and death, back home my mom and dad and I reminisced about Lois. My mother ran her fingers alongside the hem of her skirt and remarked, "There comes a time, there comes a time for all of us." In this way of acknowledging her sister's impending death, we were able to quietly mourn Lois' departure. Our good-byes to my Aunt Lois were sent via long-distance calls to Richard – which he answered in the Edinburgh ward.

After her death, Lois' body was returned to her home in Michigan, and I traveled with my family to participate in the services honoring my aunt.

When it was time for me to head home to Fargo and back to work, my cousin Paul drove me to the airport, and since timing was tight, he dropped me off at the terminal. We exchanged a quick hug and I ran to catch my flight, only to learn that it was overbooked and volunteers for a later flight were needed. Quickly checking in, I learned that I could be home only three hours later – and still in time for my next day's work – if I volunteered to be bumped.

Ah, the prize – a voucher worth $400 for a future flight! And so began my surprise "inheritance" from my Aunt Lois.

I later used that voucher as my ticket to Key West to vacation with my cousins and my sister Shirley. Cousin Gayle and I were flying from Fargo, and on the one stopover in Minneapolis, I heard the ticket agent announcing that the flight was overbooked. Quickly I moved to the counter and volunteered to be bumped. We caught a flight a half-hour later. Now I had a new "Aunt Lois" travel voucher!

Home again in Fargo, I used the voucher for a good share of my ticket cost to Hawaii to visit my niece Jill and her husband Tom. On the way home from Hawaii, in Seattle, I was alerted that the airline was overbooked, and of course I volunteered again. *Another* new "Aunt Lois" travel voucher was in my hands!

My last use of this surprise inheritance from my Aunt Lois was for half of my plane ticket to visit my paternal ancestral home in Sweden. Driving for hours deep into the hills and woods with my Swedish cousin, Anna Stina, as my guide, we found the homestead. There on the moss-covered ground of my ancestral home I marveled, delighted, and danced.

I inherited many things from my Aunt Lois – a love of reading and of color, a kinship with libraries, and a longing to see new places. Each of these inheritances has stayed with me throughout my life. But the one I remember with the most delight is the unexpected inheritance of the travel vouchers.

You could say that I've traveled nearly half-way around the world on my surprise inheritance. Each trip created new memories that brought my Aunt Lois close to me. Each gift transformed into a new gift – one that kept giving over and over again.

In Her Own Words

There are side bonuses to making a move. When I relocated from Minneapolis back to my home territory in west-central Minnesota, there was an extra benefit – the extended and leisurely times I could spend with my parents. So different from a weekend visit here and there, where time is always crunched! In those instances, there's no ease for "extra" conversations to take place. But now living in the same locale, we had space to breathe and then to pick up talks where we left off.

Perhaps no time with my mom was dearer to me than the two years at the end of her life. Dad had passed away, and I was happy to be a family companion to her. I got a kick out of her – she was a bright person, and we had fun being together. She was clear about wanting me to live my own life, and this made mine so much easier.

Decades earlier we'd had our troubles. Mom would say sometimes, speaking of my sister Shirley, brother David, and me, "You kids didn't cause us any problems or heartaches." And I'd smile and say, "Mom, don't you remember when you were going through menopause, and I was a hippie?" If she didn't remember, I did. I guess you could call those troubles the transitory kind, though. Long ago, far away, and mostly forgotten.

Mom would often ride along with me when I drove out to my tree farm. We had some great conversations. She loved clouds and would exclaim, "Oh, look at that one!" On the way back into town one day, Mom remarked: "My mother didn't want me to marry a farmer. I told your dad we couldn't marry until she had gone because I didn't want to hurt her, and then she died a week later." Mom and I glanced at each other. Mom took another peek at me and said, "That was convenient." We looked at each other again and chuckled. Mom continued, "Isn't it funny how things work out? Mother never saw the farm. She just didn't want her baby to work too hard. She remembered that a lot of farms didn't have running water. Our farm had running water from the beginning, though."

"She never made it out to the farm to see what it was like? Was she too ill?" I asked. "Yes," Mom said. "But after we were married my dad came out every Saturday, and he went straight to the garden. There was a bus from

Moorhead to Comstock, and we'd wait for him at the corner. Oh, he loved the farm!"

My mom loved the farm, too – even though she'd grown up in a city. She and Dad lived on the farm until Dad turned 80. That's when he thought it was time to move into Moorhead where snowplowing a long driveway and all the other work of a large farmstead wouldn't be necessary. They lived in a townhome for five years, and then they moved for the last five years of their life together to an independent living apartment at Riverview Place. Mom spent the last six months of her life in a memory-care apartment.

These are the snippets of conversation that I wrote down during her last two years. They touched me, and they truly captured who she was:

"Taking care of the yard, I don't call that work actually."

"I don't eat much. I'm too short to be heavy."

"And here it is – Riverview Place – where the old people live, who are young at heart."

"Oh, here I am in an old folks' home...but I qualify, darn it."

After Dad died: “I’m all alone in bed with just a pillow. No waist to put my arm around.”

“Your dad – oh, yes, he was a good man. They don’t come any better. They come richer, but not better.”

“We haven’t suffered from lack of money. We haven’t been rich, but next to it.”

Mom about Dad: “We never got into any arguments. He gave in right away.”

“You kids didn’t cause us any problems or heartaches. I thought you came home too late, but your dad would say, ‘Don’t you remember when we were young and used to go out?’”

“I never thought that the day would come that I would have an artificial Christmas tree. Here I am a farmer’s wife. I should have my head examined.”

And her thoughts on getting old:

“I’d better go – I don’t want to end up an old lady staying home all the time. The trouble is you get to a certain point and you’re happy staying put. It’s not fun to get old.”

“I have no zip – isn’t that the berries! There’s no time for that.”

Mom on traveling to Georgia to visit her granddaughter Jill and family:

"My tearing-around days are kind of over. It would be different if I was able to. There are always things to do at my place. But you go ahead! Don't think about it – just do it. You go and have a good time, and I'll get along fine."

On Mom and me living together, I said to her, "You could come to my place." Mom replied, "We should each have a place of our own."

"I want to go to my old home, you know. But here I am smiling. I want to do what you think is best for me."

"There are so many things to remember," Mom said, looking at notes left on the kitchen counter. "It's no fun to get old and forgetful. Just get old."

There's no newspaper at Mom's place today. The bill hadn't been paid. "Whoops!" I say. "That's your daughter falling down on the job." Mom responds: "That's all right, you can get up again. Don't stay down too long. We must have a few kinks in life."

Mom to me if I appear when she's not feeling good: "You're going to perk your mom up."

And her words of affirmation: “Now, you’re a smart gal. You think of the good things – not the bad.”

During a hospital stay: “I’d rather be out of here. Either home or the grave is the best place for me.”

As her health went downhill: “I’m not quite ready, but I will be when the time comes. I’ll kick the bucket and off I’ll go.”

And her last words to me: “Live life for me, Jeannie. Live life.”

A Gift to Loved Ones

I remember the conversation, and I still have the paper napkin. On it my dad had written, "If the time comes when I need to be in a nursing home, I hereby give my wholehearted consent." And then in his sprawling, loopy handwriting, he dated it and signed it, "Lynn E. Anderson, Papa."

As odd as it might sound, the conversation surrounding the signing of this napkin was jovial. Perhaps our words were casual because my family and I had discussed old age, health, and dying many times over the years. In fact, the signature on the napkin came about because during a recent conversation over a meal, Dad had made the statement about his willingness to be in a nursing home if he needed to be, and I had retorted, "I'd like that in writing, please!"

Luck in living comes in many forms, and I've found myself with more than a few lucky stars. My parents lived long, active, relatively healthy lives, each to nearly 90 years of age. Over time, we learned to speak easily about the challenges of health and shared our thoughts about death and dying. Fortunately, I was able to be with both of them when they passed on to a different world.

Dad never did end up in a nursing home; instead, he died at home under hospice care. But those conversations we had over the years gave me great grounding and some solace for the decisions that we would have to make as my parents faced the end of their lives.

Now, as I hear stories of my friends' parents facing death, I think of the ease I discovered in those discussions with my family. And I wonder: what are we learning from our parents about living and dying? What conversations, attitudes, and actions will we carry into our own older years that might be a gift to our families?

As my mom had done when her sister Lois lay dying in an Edinburgh hospital, she stroked the hem of her skirt and said, "There comes a time … there comes a time for all of us." Her gaze into the distance and then to me, coupled with her words, brought me a strange comfort.

Seven years later, she would repeat those same words to me as she lay in intensive care after suffering a couple of strokes. The neurologist and the internist were at her bedside discussing whether to initiate a clot-busting drug that might or might not lessen the effects of the stroke. The quality of her future life was unknown. That night my mom could still give us some laughter when she said slowly, with a slur, "I can barely talk and I haven't even been drinking!"

As I held my mom's hand, this time I was the one doing the stroking on the cloth of her gown. "You know," I said, "we've talked about times like this. What are you thinking now?" "Yes," she nodded, and then, again, I heard her words: "There comes a time."

"You are a remarkable family," said the doctor. But I knew it was more of a remarkable conversation, not a remarkable family. It was my mom's willingness to talk about death earlier in her life that made the end of her life so much better.

Conversations about living well and then dying well aren't necessarily easy to have, but they are critical to the well-being of those we love. Resolve to make your final wishes known as a treasured gift for your family.

CHAPTER 7

The World of Love

Prelude to Romance

It's the spare comment made by a friend, acquaintance, or sometimes even a stranger that can create a turn in one's life. At our last writer's group, the talk had shifted to relationships, and Charlotte, commenting on what life would be like without her husband Larry, said, "Oh, I'd miss the romance."

"Oh, I'd miss the romance." I'm sure that romance is only one of the things that Charlotte would miss if her husband of 40 years disappeared. However, as a long-divorced woman, I found her spontaneous words hit a soft spot in my heart. I thought, "Okay, I should go for the gold. I could use a little romance."

But at 57 years of age, how does one go for the gold? I knew that if I was super-diligent, I would take up the method prescribed in a book I'd read: make the search for love a new primary focus – other than your day job. Draw up lists of everyone you know. Ask them if they know any available men that they could introduce you to, budget dollars for spiffing up your body and your looks, and be willing to follow up with any leads you're given.

This did sound, to say the least, like a very deliberate method, and one well-suited for a planner, a driven Type A personality. So, I even considered it. Then I realized that I was more of a Type B personality, and I gave the book away to a thrift store. It was also true that when I thought of the attention and care I needed to provide for my dad and mom, my tree farm, and assorted other primary focuses beyond my day job, my drive to find a romantic companion fell by the wayside.

Every once in a while, though, the thought came back to me and even picked up speed. A friend of mine said it's a good idea to always have a crush on several people. That way, anyone that drops by the wayside because, say, he turns out to be only 40 years old, or because the woman he's with is not "just a friend," it will allow you a spare. Since then, I've found that there are many reasons for dropping someone from a crush list. I also discovered it's wise to keep a few spares in the storehouse.

Even though I was in the slow lane for love, I must have been setting myself up extremely well for romance because two years later, my long-time friend Mark asked me to travel with him up to his family-owned island in Rainy Lake, Canada. This was not the first time I'd traveled to the island with Mark. I'd known him since we met in college. We'd always had fun and a warm connection. He'd often been interested in dating me, but I didn't feel the same way. Over a week's time, though, things began shifting in my mind and heart. At a grocery store stop along the way to gather provisions, we laughed with so much hilarity that we drew attention from other shoppers. One day we sat reading, me lying on the rocks, under a big pine tree, head cushioned on a pillow, and Mark in a camping chair far away. Suddenly I wondered and I called out to him, "Have we ever lived in the same city?" From afar came his shout back, "Not since college and when we were both in Washington D.C." Hmmm. I thought. I really like this guy. I wish we lived closer.

The island was set deep into the big lake with nothing but sky, water, rocks, and forests in sight. We boated, set anchor, and meditated to the sound of water lapping and birds calling. We played Scrabble, each intent on outscoring the other and then beating each other in turn.

And then one night, while lying next to each other on the rocks — with stars twinkling, shooting, and falling above — love found a home with me at last. Could Mark be the one I'd been waiting for? I told Mark I was open to a different kind of relationship. We began to talk about whether or not we could share a future together.

On the drive home, I was at the wheel, when I turned to Mark and said, "I think we should elope." His eyes grew wide – almost like in a cartoon –- and he didn't say a word. I didn't either. I'd already said it all. Somehow, a little chuckle grew in me.

Once home, I was expecting Mark to stay overnight in the guest room at my home, as he'd done when he arrived from Washington State for the trip up to the island. Instead, once inside the condo, he grabbed his bags and said "I'll head over to Chris and Carol's now and stay the night." Talk about an abrupt departure!

Three weeks later my phone rang and there was Mark on the other end. His first words, "Do you remember what you said in the car on the way home from the island? Do you still mean that?"

"Yes, I still mean that," was my certain response. I had found romance and the man I wanted to marry.

Lucky Stars

By Mark Bratlie

Lucky stars are what we are,
One from Venus
One from Mars.
Bucking odds for common orbit,
We became binary
And couldn't be finery.
Outer space and inner space,
We manage each
With love and grace.
Our love shines brightly in the night
With warmth and joy
And healing light.
As together we grow older,
Our love twinkles
In spite of wrinkles.
We gaze on love and feel amazed.
As beauty shows,
It glows and grows.
Yes, lucky stars are what we are,
One from Venus
One from Mars.

Oh, the Joys of a Happy Marriage

It never occurred to me that my life would be expanding exponentially, and yet what a joy our marriage has been. Here's an example: Several years ago, Mark decided to put together booklets of songs and poems he'd written to give away as Christmas gifts. As a younger man, he'd entertained his nieces and nephews with his banjo playing, and now, his sister-in-law, Sharon, had suggested these songs would be a grand gift for her sons.

Prone as he was to tackling fast and furious any project that comes his way, he immediately chose, ordered, and formatted the songs and poems. Then he wrote a letter of introduction and prepared the list of family members and addresses of who would receive them. All within two days' time.

"I'll be having 50 binders made," Mark commented to me. "50!" My jaw dropped and I laughed in amazement. "If I was doing it, I'd be making only two or three." Of my immediate relatives, only two families were left: nieces Jill and Karen, their husbands and their very young children.

Later I thought, okay, if I include my brother-in-law, Al, and my close first cousins, the list would jump to 11.

This experience flashed me back to the day Mark and I first arrived at our new home, having U-Hauled and trailered his belongings from his former home in Washington State. Though initially tired, we suddenly sprang to life and started redecorating what had been my home, adding Mark's paintings, sculptures, and photos to the walls. One that went up was a framed photo of his family, taken on his mom's 90th birthday. My eyes could barely take it all in. "It's a tribe!" I exclaimed. There, in the large photo in front of me, stood 63 people gathered together. Call it the "Clan of the Bratlies" if you like.

Then I recalled the reception after my mother's funeral. She and I were the last members of my birth family, and now she was physically absent. I stopped at a table to greet someone, who exclaimed, "Oh, now you're all alone." "No, I'm not all alone!" I spoke back. Something in me rejected the "all alone" concept. I had friends and family, just not the immediate kind of family in the large numbers that some people have. I didn't feel all alone, and I didn't want that label.

At our wedding, my cousin Jane said to Mark and me: “This is a marriage made in Heaven.”

And now I think she was right. All the family who cared for me and hoped for such a marriage for me had gone on to another world — where they could help arrange it. And so, it happened.

Nor Even

By Mark Bratlie

Each other together:
What could be better?
Not money
Not fame
Nor a second house in Maine.
Not a warm coat
Not a top hat
Nor even a loving cat.
Not cupcakes
Not a Learjet
Nor a most stunning sunset.
Not vacations
Not a free pass
Nor even first class.
Not a diamond
Not a jewel
Nor a multi-purpose tool.
Not a good read
Not a new tune

Nor a pair of laughing loons.
Not morning coffee
Not a warm scone
Nor even an end to this poem!

From Grumpy to Grateful

It's the natural world that opens me up. It's the first step that propels me forward. Sometimes I have to make myself go outside because I know that movement and outdoor light are what I need. In some of those instances, I say to myself, "Go! Get outside! If you want to turn back in three minutes, you can." Oddly enough, I can't think of any time that I've ever turned back.

At home, we weren't always happy with each other – Mark could be off in his world and I in mine. The slightest bit of testiness filled the space between us. Plus, the space between us in our condo wasn't always quite large enough.

The space had certainly seemed large enough earlier in the day, but that was because I was alone. And later, walking home from church, the world was wide open and balmy. Winter snowmelt was dripping from railings and roofs, and birds were singing oh so cheerily. I did a double trek around the park, just because I could.

Now that I was home though, the delight had left and a kind of grumpiness set in.

"Outdoors! Outdoors! For the both of us," I thought. As though a mom were shooing us out, we left our condo. At first we ambled along, but almost immediately we sped up as we spied the wisps of clouds streaking across the sky. The first half-hour left Mark remarking that his knee was aching and me re-adjusting my lumpy woolen sock, but then I said, "Oh, let's go on a ways farther."

There was life all around us along the dike and the river: children sliding on saucers, dogs, bikes, joggers, strollers, and cross-country skiers. Some things were hidden from sight but still caught our ears – from across the river, a soft "Who, who, whooo" called to us again and again.

It was half-way back that I turned to Mark and, respecting his modest nature, I said, "No one can see us – let's kiss." And on his lips, I planted a good firm "I love you" kiss. I couldn't resist. The outdoors had once again re-energized and transformed me.

How did this happen? I'd lumbered out, strolled along, cantered up and down a dike, seen the late afternoon moon rising in the sky, noted the U-turn that a tree limb had taken, and taken that same U-turn myself. And on the way I'd propelled myself from grumpy to grateful.

The Motel Lottery

My eyes opened wide, as my husband Mark and I pulled into the parking lot at the motel in International Falls. Cars and pickups filled nearly all the spaces. Clusters of men stood about chatting. Their bright yellow highway vests and construction gear shone with spots of color in the fading evening light.

Checking in at the front desk, I asked the receptionist, "With the rooms that remain, what might be the quietest option?" Her fingers flipped through the tall reservation cards, and with surprise she exclaimed, "You're in 201, the Jacuzzi room! That's on the second floor, way at the end of the hallway. It faces trees, not the parking lot. I'm sure it will be quiet." And then a few seconds later, "Oh, I see, you have an upgrade."

An upgrade? I wondered how we could possibly upgrade from a Jacuzzi room. She said, "Your charge will be $65. It's usually $109." She paused, "That's in my boss's handwriting."

"Well then," I said, "it must be the truth! It looks like we won the motel lottery." We laughed with pleasure.

"Yes, you did," she said, and she waved us up and away.

Mark and I marveled at our good fortune as we toted our suitcases up the steps and around the corner to our room. Not quite knowing what to expect, we opened the door to find a huge suite. A comfy sofa sat adjacent to a big white Jacuzzi.

We looked at each other in wonder. I moved quickly to the two large maroon-curtained areas and pulled the cord of one. Outside were trees whose leaves had just begun to turn to the golds and reds of fall. The second curtain opened to the same spectacle. Stepping back and looking left, I saw another large room where a queen-sized bed stood. Carved into the blonde headboard were two moose and many evergreen trees.

Our bodies were deeply tired from six hours of car travel on top of an overly busy week. We hesitated little before turning the tub stopper and the knobs of the Jacuzzi to let the water flow. Shedding our clothes, we stepped in. Ah! We could lie at full length facing each other, and the soft towels cushioned our heads. Our bodies relaxed in the whirl of the water. We were so happy in each other's company.

That mesmerizing pleasure at the beginning of our stay lingered through the night, as we held and cuddled each other. We awoke two times, once with knee pain and another with cold, but we were easily able to remedy those dilemmas, and we slid back into sleep.

Our eyes opened at first light, but we turned and cozied deeper into the bliss that had held us during the night. Twelve hours of sleep was a grace gift. Our stay proved a blessing for the week to come.

Seasons of Promise
Song by Mark Bratlie
Inspired by Jean Anderson

Winter is a time of warmth when I am close to you
A time of sharing stories and of praising what is true
The cold wind can be daunting when one is all alone
But Winter is a time of warmth when I am close to you

Spring is filled with wonderment when I am close to you
A time of bursting energy and life so bold and new
The rain can be quite chilling when one is all alone
But Spring is filled with wonderment when I am close to you

I will be with you in Winter when snow is thick and cold
I will be with you in Springtime when new life is taking hold
I will be with you in Summer when sun and growth abound
I will be with you when Autumn's old life decorates the ground

Summer's light is restful when I am close to you
As nature paints a picture with pleasing greens and blue
The heat can be exhausting when one is all alone
But Summer's light is restful when I am close to you

Autumn days are crisp and clear when I am close to you
The reds and golds come once again, yet always seem so new
Letting go brings sadness when one is all alone
But Autumn days are crisp and clear when I am close to you

I will be with you in Winter when snow is thick and cold
I will be with you in Springtime when new life is taking hold
I will be with you in Summer when sun and growth abound
I will be with you when Autumn's old life decorates the ground

CHAPTER 8

A Changing World of Love

Do You Know Her?

"You sure have more appointments than anybody I know," my husband Mark exclaimed to me. And then with a shrug of his shoulders, a smile, and a shine in his eyes, he added in his easy-going manner, "But that's all right."

He was standing in the parking lot alongside Alyce — the co-owner of BeeHive Homes of Moorhead, a memory care home — and I was sitting in our car. I was due to depart the next day for a week's solo vacation up on the rocky shores of Lake Superior, and I would have found it extremely hard to leave without seeing him first.

But that was treacherous for me, at least emotionally. It had been almost a year since Mark had moved into BeeHive Homes. The past months had been laced with panic, grief, and relief. A bit of panic with the pandemic, great grief over the loss of my husband's bright mind, and sweet relief that other people — fresh to work from their other lives — were there to help Mark with all the tasks of everyday living.

While I couldn't bear to escape to the North Shore of Lake Superior before saying good-bye, I also couldn't imagine spending an hour with him and then slithering away. Most times my departures were hard on him and hard on me. A friend suggested it would be okay to go away without a visit with Mark, saying "He wouldn't remember anyway if it was yesterday or a week ago that you were together." That was likely true, but still…I couldn't skip my good-bye.

So, I had called Alyce, who was an RN skilled in compassion, memory issues, and with a heart for Mark. I wanted any comment she might have on my dilemma. She suggested a drive-by. Oh, yes! I'd done that a couple of times during the pandemic when restrictions were tight. I'd go get one of Mark's favorite drinks, and then drive over and settle into the parking lot of the building where he now lived. Out would come Alyce and Mark, and we'd visit in the open air from a safe distance. Silly conversations, some nonsensical and some zany and bright with humor, would ensue and then I'd be off. Off because, as Alyce would say, "Jean has an appointment she has to get to."

It was a relatively easy way for me to see Mark and have the pleasure of being together, but also to avoid the collision of emotions that happened to both of us with longer visits, and the residue of sadness that would follow those departures.

We'd married late in life, after other marriages and after decades of long-distance friendship. A number of years ago, an invitation from Mark to spend time together on a wooded island in Rainy Lake, Canada, led hopeful friends to suggest that maybe Mark and I would become a couple. "Not a chance," I said. I knew it wasn't going to happen. But then, mesmerized by the calling loons, falling stars, and northern lights, love blossomed.

We hadn't been married that long — just seven years — when I noticed that odd occurrences started to take place in Mark's daily life. An inability to grasp directions to a local store, buying a birthday card for "an uncle" when Mark was actually the uncle. And then a cry came out of him on several mornings, "What is happening to my brain?"

When had these changes started? Driving back from the cornfields of Nebraska after a glorious time watching the full solar eclipse, I realized that Mark couldn't make sense of the road map. As a frequent driver of back-country roads, I was frustrated and couldn't understand. How hard could it be to read a map? Apparently, very hard.

This wasn't the first time that things seemed a bit unusual, but I discounted much of it to Mark's whimsical, absent-minded personality. I often called him "Mr. Summa Cum Laude" and "My Renaissance Man" – for more than any other person I knew, he took his interests and polished them into talents: ventriloquism, banjo strumming, harmonica playing, poetry writing, and stained-glass work — all this on top of his lifelong work as an educator. He also had a sharp wit. Mark's defining comment about his arc from teaching kindergarten kids to teaching men in prison was: "I was always hoping that one of the men wouldn't say, 'Oh, Mr. Bratlie, I remember you! You were my kindergarten teacher'."

Yet more and more often now, there were signs of something amiss. "Aren't we going to meditate?" Mark asked. "We just did," I replied. Again, from Mark while lying in bed, "I get mixed up easily when there's too much stuff happening." And one time when calling me from his stained-glass studio, "I don't know where my phone is." Oh? "Mark, you're talking on it!" We made light of it and laughed, but I hurt a little inside. And a warning bell went off. Perhaps one of the last defining incidents occurred one morning when I found him in bed crying out, "Nobody has told me what I'm supposed to do!" More and more now, Mark needed direction in all things.

I was exhausted. Mark couldn't bear to have me out of his sight. It turns out that Mark wasn't the only one losing his mind. I was too — but in a different way. And we were both scared.

The thought came to me early one morning as I stood in the room where one of Mark's stained glass creations shone bright in all its glory: "Mark needs a new place to live." That thought startled me by its sudden appearance, but a day later it was still there. And I was no longer startled.

Several years ago, there was an initial brush-off from the doctors we consulted. The mini-mental test in his primary doctor's office found only a minor skip in his math countdown. I was dismayed. "But something isn't right!" I protested to his doctor. My firm and repeated insistence caused the doctor to suggest that we could try consulting a neuropsychologist for further testing. Which we did. But that too resulted in a summary, after a morning-long battery of tests, that "Mark is very smart, but just a little slow and deliberate. The only thing that shows up odd is his spatial grasp, and it seems hard to believe he could still be doing stained glass with that issue." Once again, my refusal to believe such a rosy prognosis came to the forefront. "Well, then, something is wrong with me," I said, "because things are just so different." His recommendation: Simplify. Simplify. Simplify.

We did just that to the best of our ability, but the stealthy disease of dementia kept up its relentless pace.

All of the things that Mark so desperately needed in his life — continual attention and routine — I could perhaps provide, but they were taking the life out of me. And in actuality, try as I might, I really couldn't provide the quality of care Mark truly needed for his well-being. I was deluding myself to think I could.

Sometimes we get lucky in life. And I was lucky the morning that Mark's brother Dave and wife Sharon sat with us on our balcony. My own health concerns had come to the forefront, and now Dave took the lead in explaining to Mark that I'd asked him and Sharon for help in finding a place where Mark might live while I regained my health.

"Would you like to see the room we've found?" Dave asked. "No, I trust you," Mark commented. My body, which had been trembling in anticipation of this talk began to calm, and I said, "I know this is going to be very tough for each of us, but I hope we can rise to the occasion." From his chair, Mark began to rise and he uttered these words: "I think we can rise to the occasion." My heart leapt. And just a few seconds later he added: "I will do whatever I can in order to help Jean." Tears began to roll down my face and I turned to him saying, "That's almost the best gift you've ever given me." His tenderness and kindness overwhelmed me.

It turned out that my solo trip to the North Shore of Lake Superior was wonderful. I sat on the rocks and watched the calm water, the wild waves, and the swooping birds. I also walked and read a lot. I was soothed. I booked a cabin for next year.

And on my return, it was fun and tender to rejoin Mark. He'd done well with a visit from his brother Dave, plus a friend or two. The superb care of the BeeHive Home people also helped him feel secure while I was away.

After lunch on Friday, we were going to head out for a drive and a mocha when he paused outside his door, looked around a bit, and said, “I wonder where Jean is.” Perhaps I asked, “Jean?” as I thought to myself, “Is there another Jean here at BeeHive?” I must have had a quizzical look on my face because he said, “Yes, Jean Anderson.” My hand started moving to my throat and I was about to say, “That’s me!” when I thought better of it and said simply, “Oh”.

“Do you know her?” he asked. And then, “Do you like her?” In a moment of great self-affirmation, I said, “Yes! I like her a lot. What about you?” Mark searched my face intently for a few seconds and then said with a big smile, “Yes, but not as much as I like you.”

Oh my. Clearly that is a tale of mistaken identity. Or a brain caught in a maze. Or the depth of Mark’s love for me.

Now, as the months go by, I’m the one searching his face for the real Mark. He’s there, I know, but now an ever-changing mystery to me. As each new Mark emerges,

I dig deep, looking for more ways to see and love the next Mark hidden inside.

Beyond the Tears

How do you explain the inexplicable? You don't. That's the glory and purpose of certain gems of mystery. The "whys" of them remain in the realm of the unknown – a part of the world hidden to us. Often appearing during crossroads in our lives, at times most chaotic or most still, they open us up to a wider world. Here's how one worked for me.

Imagine this scene: Mark and I are driving back to town after an extremely short foray to our farm. He is deep into his struggle with dementia, and now is living full-time in memory care at BeeHive Homes.

Less than two minutes after we get out of the car at our country place, Mark comments: "I don't want to stay here too long." I'm surprised and taken aback, but I want him to be at ease as we make our way to the newly planted garden. "Oh, Mark," I say, "we'll go right back! Let me just pull off the sheets I used to protect the plants from the freeze last night. Then we'll head back."

In the past, the drives to and from our spot in the country were always one of our favorite things to do. The big open sky, the clouds, the fields of black soil or new green growth – such a source of pleasure. Not to mention our beloved glass-sided gazebo that let all the outside come inside.

Now, getting back in the car, Mark touches his abdomen and moans. He had tried to use the bathroom in the garden shed, but his mind is so mixed up that the place is now unfamiliar, dark, and scary to him. When he tries to button his shirt to the belt of his jeans, I determine that we should leave immediately. I ask Mark and he agrees. Once in the car, thankfully he nods off as we begin the ride back to his home at BeeHive.

At the corner of the gravel road and highway, I text Mark Goldthorpe, the co-owner of BeeHive Homes: "Can we get help right away? Bathroom? We're about 30 minutes away."

"Yep, I will let them know. I'm heading over too. You might beat me."

In the meantime, Mark snoozes on. A kind of quiet desperation comes over me as I try to balance the need for speed, the hope that Mark won't wake, and the stone-solid realization that never again will Mark and I be coming out together to our country place. Those days are over. The wide-open space of the land and the sky is overwhelming to him now. He doesn't feel comfortable or safe. So much has changed. So much is gone.

Tears flow down my face. This is tough. The passage of time reveals the vitality draining away from him. And our cherished times together in the country are now gone too.

It's full speed ahead until we hit the intersection south of Moorhead. Instead of a green light, I see yellow and then watch it turn to red. Oh. No! Just let me get Mark back to his home. Why this stoplight? Why now?

Yet as I cry, I spy this unusual word on the license plate of the car right in front of us: no numbers, just the word **PRAISE**. Praise? Yes, Praise. How ridiculous, I think, and yet there it is like a big billboard dropped smack down in my sight. Praise. There's nothing to do but take it in. I'm stopped in traffic. I pause and think, "Yes, Praise. Praise for what? *Praise for all that has been*. I can do that."

Yes, Praise. Yes, Tears. Yes, Praise. Yes, Tears. Yes, Praise.

At BeeHive, one of our favorite workers, Mason, comes out waving. Mark looks over, lights up, and waves back. "Oh look Mark, here's our friend Mason." He comes around to Mark's side of the car: "Let's go in and get you to the bathroom. We can go in the side door. Here, we'll cut across." Mason puts an arm around Mark's shoulder and leads him in.

Later as I leave, the tears return and meditation comes to mind. I recall how I asked Mark, because he seemed to be a meditation pro, "What do you do with tears during meditation?"

"Just keep breathing, let them come and return to breathing," he'd reply.

And now on this day, "Just keep breathing" is what I do. Tears. Breathing. Praise. Breathing. Tears. Breathing. Praise. Breathing. I will carry on.

This Is What He Does

"Does Mark still recognize you?" my friend Marlene asks. The question sets me off. This is the one thing that people always ask me now. I have to fight off being irate. It puts me on the spot.

My voice is strained: "My standard answer, Marlene, is 'Yes, he does, but in a different way than before'." And then I go on to being my cranky self: "Why is this the question that people *always* ask me now? I know I'm being short with you about it. I'm sorry this is the way that I'm responding."

She is kind enough to say, "I take it as a compliment that you can speak this way to me. It means we're family and friends. You feel safe saying this to me."

We go deeper into it. I tell her I hate the fact that I respond so selfishly when I hear this question. But it's always right off: "How is Mark doing? Does Mark recognize you?" I stiffen up. "Why is it all about Mark? Why aren't people asking how *I'm* doing?" As I'm saying this, I realize how pathetic I sound.

"But it *is* a way of asking about you," she replies. "I think that's what people are really asking when they ask those questions; they're really asking out of concern for you and how you're doing," Marlene says. "People ask this question because when they think of dementia and Alzheimer's, most of us think that the worst and most horrible thing would be— if it happened to someone we love— that they would no longer recognize us. That the person wouldn't know us."

Really? I never thought of it that way. From now on, I'll have to put on that shield when I hear the question.

And now to answer that question— "Does Mark recognize you?"— No. He no longer spies me from across the community room, lights up, opens his arms wide, and dances towards me. No, he no longer speaks my name and gives me a big hug.

But there is still a lot of Mark there … here! This is what he does: he looks at me long and hard; he sometimes brightens with tenderness and a smile; he sometimes says, "You look great!" And last Sunday he placed his hand on my shoulder and kept it there.

This is the Mark that I hold in my heart and in my mind.

And now I understand the real reason why I respond so coldly to the question, "Does Mark recognize you?" It's because I have to go back in my mind to remember when he recognized me in the manner in which people are asking. Then I have to make the transition to how he recognizes me now. Then I have to realize the loss … again.

Realizing the loss all over again is not something that I want to do. But I have learned that my mission in bearing witness to Mark and to this disease is to face it—to feel its pain and sorrow, to embrace its beauty and tenderness, and then to shake off the gloom and doom – and live.

Breathe in peace, breathe out pain.
Breathe in peace, breathe out pain.
Breathe in peace, breathe out peace.

This is my mission. It's my way to honor Mark's life … and my own.

Hard Talk
By Mark Bratlie

Love you
and love to talk freely
(while shadows lurk inside)

Trust you
and feel so uneasy
(being vulnerable terrifies)

Sharing with you
dark parts of me
(afraid you will love me less)

Wanting you
to know the real me
(putting it to the test)

Risking with you
and laying it bare
(hoping you come to my aid)

Holding you
and feeling quite safe
(as shadows start to fade)

The Send-Off

Spoken at Mark's Prayer Service

My gentle-spirited husband Mark died, as all of us would want to, surrounded by love. His brother Dave and wife Sharon were at his bedside. They had encouraged me to go home and get some rest. And so it happened that Mark slipped away after I had slipped away.

It was a bright blue, beautiful June-sky day – with puffy white clouds floating by – the kind he loved to watch and name: "Oh, look! There's a poodle!"

Yup, that was my husband – airy, otherworldly, and oh…so many other things.

We'd met in an encounter group led by Pastor Carl Lee at Concordia College. That was a group where you could share life experiences and feelings. It was the Sixties, you know! We stayed friends throughout the decades, and through both of our marriages, mine and his. And whenever we'd get together for visits, one of our friends would inevitably say to me, "Oh, maybe someday you and Mark will become a couple." And my quick response was, "Not a chance. It's not going to happen." Of that I was certain. Mark was like a brother to me. Shows you how much I knew.

And then one summer he invited me again to the family island in Canada. Over that week's time, my heart turned. Lucky me.

Long after that, I wrote Mark a note telling him what he and our marriage had brought to my life:

a wry, fun, and silly sense of humor

a wider political perspective

nearly a decade of travel to a magical secluded nature spot – the island at Rainy Lake

a big family – his eight sisters and brothers who took me in and claimed me as their own

the beauty of stained-glass art, poetry, banjo tunes, and harmonica music

a gazebo or two

perseverance

a living example of how to use your God-given talents.

When Mark's illness began to impact his spatial abilities, and he had to close his Turtle Shell Stained Glass

Studio, I wondered how we would carry on. We did by starting what we called the Stained Glass Tour – trips to different businesses, churches, and homes where Mark's stained-glass art had been installed. It was a wonderful way to honor his work, to have fun traveling together, and to move on despite his disease.

One of my favorite stories from that time happened at an airport, after Mark realized he'd left his hat behind on the plane. And he was a hat man. "Oh, I'm sure we can find another in one of the stores," I said. And we did. It was a perfect hat for Mark. Blue, his favorite color, and with "You Betcha" embroidered on top of the visor. Up to the counter Mark went to pay. The clerk rang up the purchase and then asked, "Would you like a bag for your hat?" Skipping nary a beat, Mark looked up and said, "No, I have a head." A moment passed and laughter broke out.

Yes, I was a lucky woman to have Mark nearly always in my life, and for thirteen years to have him as my husband.

Thank you for coming to his farewell. Thank you for surrounding me and the rest of Mark's and my family during this time of sorrow. Your love holds us up.

Peace Recipe

By Mark Bratlie

Letting be and letting go
are skills that we can nourish
And when we do we set the stage
for peace within to flourish

This life is full of changes
that we cannot control
And fighting this reality
is bound to take a toll

To grasp and cling to good times
brings anxiety and fear
Which can block out full enjoyment
even while good times are here

Bitter fighting with the bad times
merely feeds them energy
While letting go of constant struggle
tends to set one's spirit free

If we can let life come and go
we will be much more at peace
Not only on the outside
but way down underneath

CHAPTER 9

A Few Good Men

Lightening the Load

I was recently touched by the story of a man who had been fired from work during the holiday season. He was despondent but not bitter, and he vowed that should his fortunes ever change, he would make this season a special time for others.

An entrepreneur at heart and by skill, he eventually grew wealthy, and he began a tradition of giving $100 bills out to certain people he noticed as appearing to be in need. He simply handed them an envelope with the bill inside, said "Merry Christmas," and quietly left the premises.

I've long pondered this story.

Like most of us, I've had my share of similar small experiences. Once while pulling into the parking lot at my home, I noticed an older gentleman looking a little bedraggled, pawing at the coin returns along a row of newspaper stands in search of any coins left at the bottom. His actions gave me pause, and I watched him for a moment or two.

Then I reached for my purse, grabbed the few bills and change available, and walked over to him. "Here you go, sir," I said. He looked at what I'd given him, then up at me in surprise. He grabbed my shoulders, pulled me to him and kissed me on the forehead, saying "Bless you, bless you." Tears came into his eyes, and only then did I notice his ballpark cap that said "WWII Vet."

His blessing of so many years ago left its mark on my forehead — and in my heart. Since then, whenever I can, I again try to be aware of the stranger in need.

A few years later, while driving to work on a windy snowy morning, I noticed a slightly bent figure trudging down the walkway by the underpass below the railroad tracks. Something unusual caught my eye. His rounded shoulders, flat-footed steps, clothes a bit worn and limp all reminded me a bit of my dear departed brother. I turned to catch a better look as I drove past him on the street and saw that, although he was young, he seemed heavily burdened.

What could I do to lighten his load? My mind scurried to think of or find something for him. Cash? As I recalled, my billfold at the moment was empty. I said a prayer. "Think, think," I murmured to myself. Then I remembered the roll of quarters I had tucked in my car's glove compartment.

But I'd already driven past him, and the streets didn't seem to be cooperating – the one-way I was on led to another one-way, and back-tracking to get to him would be tricky. But three minutes later, I saw him. Pulling over on a side street and jumping out of my car, I called to him, "Sir, sir!" He glanced around to see where the shouts were coming from. Moving toward him, I motioned for him to come my way. He must have wondered what could I possibly want from him?

He came close and I saw that yes, he was indeed young – maybe 17 – with beautiful dark brown clear eyes. "I just wanted to wish you a Merry Christmas," I said, and I handed over the roll of quarters to his gloveless hands. Our eyes held each other's eyes for a long moment. And then we each turned and went our own way.

Once back in my car, I paused and saw him proceeding across the street. He turned back one time when he was about a half-block away, and he gazed in my direction. Each of us was wondering, "What just happened there?" In the space of five minutes, each of our lives had changed a small bit.

Then the blessing came back to me again. As he turned back to continue his walking, his shoulders straightened, his step lightened, and so, I hope, did the world around him. My world certainly did.

A Good Man

It's always been men. I've seen men crossing the bridge over the Red River, standing at bus stops or street corner stop lights, or hurrying along a street that has no sidewalk. Strange that it's never been women I've noticed, but only men.

They stick out because they stride hard, or stand with hands jammed in their pockets, or keep their shoulders hunched up. They're bolstering themselves against the wicked winter north wind of 22 miles an hour and minus 5 degrees temperatures. One look at them and you shiver.

Maybe it all started when my dad and I were driving in his pickup one day, and we passed an old church serving as a homeless shelter. Dad turned to me and said, "I'm afraid David might end up homeless someday." Oh. That was a tough admission to hear from Dad. My brother David never did end up homeless, but it opened my heart for people who might be.

Winters can be dreadfully — even deadly — cold in Fargo-Moorhead. There's no lingering to be had without significant clothing, or you risk serious damage to life and limbs. The relentless wind, snow, and freezing temperatures could kill you.

One January Sunday morning found me winding my way to see my husband Mark at his memory care home. The sky was muted still in its night darkness, but it was brightened subtly by the snow and streetlights. Freezing cold. A frozen world. Minus 13 degrees!

And who is that walking past the roundabout onto the bridge? At this time, on this day, in this bleak mid-winter? I slow down… I turn to look at him. I catch his eyes…and I wonder… who is out here in this weather? The earth frozen solid in its stillness. There is no traffic yet. The light so soft and the day so still on what is normally a full and fast-paced bridge.

I slow…I wonder…no traffic. Not a car in sight. Offer him a ride, I think. But what if he pulls a gun? I almost laugh at myself. Out of his pocket he would pull a gun? Not likely.

There are snowbanks piled along the side of the road. He'd have to climb over. Slow…slow I go. And now a break in the snowbanks. He looks at me. I motion

"Come!" And I still keep driving slowly. He begins a slow trot to meet me. I put on the car blinkers to warn others. I see a couple of headlights in the deep distance. My car door is locked. So I unlock it.

He gets in. Sweet relief. "Thank you," he utters.

"Yes," I say, "It's too cold out there. Where are you going?"

"To Burger King."

"What's your name?"

"Doug."

"My name is Jean."

He's now squeezed into the front seat. I'd tossed everything I could into the back. Then I noticed his hands. Red, ice white. Bare. No gloves!

"Here, try these on." I pulled off my gloves and handed them to him.

"They're your gloves."

"Yes, but you need gloves."

Doug tries, but he can't pull them on. Too small.

I see that Walgreen's is ahead. "I'm going to pull in here. You need some gloves."

There is a perceptible pause. “I don’t have any money.”

“That doesn’t matter. You need gloves.” Usually, I’ve had a stash in the backseat of my car, plus scarves and hats. Where are they?

Slowly we go into Walgreen’s parking lot, but they’re not open.

“Where were you walking from?”

“The other side of downtown.”

I simply can’t imagine it. He has a stocking cap, a hoodie pulled over that. Tennis shoes — not boots — and a semi-serious winter jacket, but NO GLOVES.

On to more snippets of conversation. He’s already told me he thinks a contractor will call with work for him. But he’s still $100 short of his rent money. He’ll do anything…shovel snow…I ask for his phone number and gave him mine.

Just down the street is Hornbacher’s grocery. It’s open. “I’m going to swing in here for a minute. Why don’t you come in?” In the parking lot, I’m thinking…haven’t I seen gloves in here? Walking towards the store, Doug says again, “I don’t have any money on me.”

"Oh, that's okay." And from Doug, "I'm so ashamed. I'm 28…a grown man."

"Oh, don't think twice! Everybody needs help at some time. I've needed help. I'm just passing it along."

In the store, I head directly left and spy the rack at the end of an aisle. "There it is — pick out some gloves." Doug tries on one or two and finds a pair that pulls on easily. I'm casting my eyes over the rack…anything else of use? "Get another pair." And so, he pulls on a gray fleece set. Then I spy a balaclava mask. "Would this be helpful for your face?" "Yes," he says, and over we go to check-out. I request an extra $50 from the cashier.

Back in the car. But all of a sudden, I think of his $100 need for rent. "Let's go back in for a minute. I'm going to get a mocha for my husband. Would you like something?"

While we're ordering at the kiosk, Doug says, "I can't read the sign." Hmmm, I wonder, maybe he can't see well, maybe he can't read. I'll get him the same as I do for Mark, a medium turtle mocha. Then I tell Doug I'll be back in a minute. I head to the ATM and pull $100 out. When I return to the coffee kiosk, our drinks are soon ready and out we go to the car where our conversation continues.

I'm quietly startled when Doug discloses a painful memory.

"It was $6,000 for my mom's burial. My sister had $5,000 and I had $500. My mother had a necklace. I have it now. It has a gold charm with the letter S for Sharon. I don't want to sell it."

"Of course. You can't sell it. When did she die?"

"Two weeks ago." Oh!

"Was it expected?"

"No, she died during the night. Accidental overdose of pain meds. Oxygen just kept going down. I don't know why I came here. A couple of friends here."

"Good friends?" I ask.

"No. Not quite the same goals as I have."

"What are yours?"

"Find good work. Get married. Get a cabin for our home."

We arrive at Burger King. I've told him earlier about Mark — how he's on hospice care but keeps on living. I now tell him, “I’m so sorry about your loss. That’s very tough.” Doug replies, “She was only 58.”

Doug gets out and sets his mocha on the pavement. “My friend is waiting for me, so I guess I better put these on.” He pulls the gloves apart, picks up the tag that’s fallen to the ground, and then puts on the gloves.

The $100 I have is folded, and I put the $50 with it. Leaning over the passenger seat, I hand it to him. “Here, I want you to have this for your rent.” Doug’s whole body stops. “Oh,” he utters. I see his face contort and the beginning of tears. “Oh.” He is without words. I don’t want to delay the moment. “God bless you,” I say. A pause.

He looks at me, “God bless you!”

Another Good Man

It seems like these adventures always start with a bit of a delay, and then a sudden decision to get moving. I was going to take a nap before departing to visit our farm, and I lay down on the sofa, but after just a bit I thought, "I've got to get going!" So up I went. I'd made my to-go lunch earlier, so I was all set. "I can rest at the farm," I thought.

Backing out of the garage, my eyes noticed something odd by the small, tunneled side door entrance. A planter or pot? It looked like a large brown polished vase with some rumpled cloth nearby.

I pulled up. I usually head out in the other direction, but now I pulled over to check this out. I was curious.

It was a man lying curled up in a tight ball on the cement landing! Getting out of the car, I stepped towards him. After all he was, so to speak, at my doorstep.

"Sir! Sir, are you all right?" I hoped he wasn't dead.

He roused, unfolded slightly, and then looked up at me. "Yes, but I'm so cold." He was dressed in hot-summer wear — shorts and a t-shirt.

"Would you like a shirt or covering or something?" At the last minute before leaving the condo, I'd pulled my husband's favorite farm-mowing shirt from the closet. A big white linen shirt that I loved seeing Mark in. It hadn't been worn or out of the closet in nearly a year since Mark had been ill, and I'd wanted to have a part of Mark with me when I was at the farm. I pulled it from the car and handed it to this unusual man. He pulled it close like a cape over his chest and shoulders.

"Are you thirsty?"

"Yes!" I had a bottle of water on the front car seat, and I brought it to him.

"Would you like something to eat?" He nodded.

"I'll go get something. A sandwich?"

"Yes," he replied.

"What else would you like?"

"Fruit." Fruit? I thought. That seems like a request Mark would make.

"I'll be right back. If someone comes, tell them Jean has gone to get something for you." He nodded.

"I'm Michael. Michael Stone. I'm from Turtle Mountain."

"Were you here all night?" I asked, rather incredulously.

"Most of it. I got lost in the park and thought I could stay out of any rain here."

I jumped into my car and pulled it to the back parking lot, and then I ran upstairs to get food. In the fridge I found the remaining half of a cantaloupe. Fruit. Then I quickly defrosted some bread and made a peanut butter sandwich. The remaining fabulous spicy nuts that my cousins Carlene and Phil had given to me went into a container. I found a $20 bill in my cash stash and returned to Michael with a plastic set of silverware and a napkin. All tucked in a to-go bag.

"God bless you," I heard as I arrived. Michael started to rise up.

"No, no. You don't need to leave." I showed him the food. "Here are some nuts and a peanut butter sandwich. And some fruit."

"You could have called the police. Most people would have called the police."

I looked at Michael. "If I had felt threatened by you or frightened, I would have called the police." But clearly, he was no threat to me.

The previous evening I'd been reading about the statue created by Timothy P. Schmalz, placed temporarily at St. Mary's Basilica in Minneapolis: *Angels Unawares. "Do not neglect to show hospitality, for you may be entertaining angels unawares." (Hebrews 13:2 King James Version)*

And here he was. An angel right in front of me!

"My husband Mark used to teach kindergarten at Turtle Mountain," I said. "Do you want to go back to Turtle Mountain?"

"I could but I'm trying to find some work here in town. I would do anything. My dad died two years ago. My brother died. My mother isn't doing so good."

Our conversation continued, and though Michael was dressed right for a hot summer day, it seemed a bit skimpy for the cool morning air. "Could you use a jacket and a backpack?" I asked. He nodded.

"Okay, stay here and I'll be back." Up the stairs I went again, this time pulling Mark's travel backpack that I hadn't yet given away, plus several shirts and a lightweight jacket. I rolled the shirts and tucked them into the backpack. Grabbed a couple of Kleenex packs, the $20 bill, a few tins of pineapple, applesauce, an apple, banana, and more nuts. And then I headed back downstairs. As I handed Michael the jacket, he passed Mark's linen shirt back to me. I helped him get the rain jacket on over his head.

"Can I give you a ride somewhere?"

"No, I'm okay. Is it just through the park to the shelter?"

"Yes. Would you like a prayer of passage?" I asked.

"Yes, please," he said and bowed his head. I was tempted to put my hand on his head but refrained. I spoke a prayer of peace. Michael was now prepared for his journey, and I was prepared for mine — thanks to his angelic appearance in my life.

The Train That Delayed Me

I'm waiting for the train to pass when I spy the man at the corner by the Dairy Queen. The traffic can't move ahead. He is trudging along. His feet barely pick up. Truly, he looks beyond weary.

I think of all of us buzzing around in our cars — a holiday weekend about to begin. And there he is — a lone figure with a heavy pack on his back. Trudge. Trudge. Trudge.

Is there anything I could do? Interesting now when I think about it. I didn't offer him a ride. But I did pull out some $2 bills that I'd just brought to tuck into the car console.

A block and a half later I caught up with him as we waited at another stoplight. There's a parking lot right on the corner, and I pull into it.

"Sir, sir!" He looks up and over, and I beckon to him. "You look weary. Can I offer you something so you can get food or drink?" He nods, "Yes".

I hand the folded-up bills his way. He perks up! His eyes brighten as he looks down. He's looking at the bills as he pulls them to his chest. His shoulders lift. He smiles at me and waves.

I'm once again struck by how being in the right place at the right time can open your heart and make the best connections where you'd least expect them.

Golden Glowing Gloves

The young man's hands are jammed in his pockets. Shoulders hunched up against the relentless cold north winter wind. His coal black skin and manner of dress — very little — makes me think he's new to this country. I can't go anywhere. The stoplight holds me up. Hmmm. What to do?

I reach into the back seat for my bag of gloves. One pair left, not yet given away. Super-warm, golden-glowing deerskin gloves with fleece lining. I tear off the tag. Pull the car forward. Catch his eyes and hold up the gloves, with a question on my face. "Need these?"

He nods, "Yes!" Over the snowbank he steps. My window rolls down. Gloves held out the window. Again, a nod from him, "Thank you!" He steps back over the snow and pulls them on. Hands now outside of his pockets. He glances down at them.

His shoulders straighten. The light turns green. Off I drive with a smile. He is standing tall. Glowing golden hands at his side.

CHAPTER 10

Digging In or Reaching Out

Could We Step Back, Please?

When I heard the shouts, "Lock her up. Lock her up!" I thought: "Could we step back, please?" I couldn't cry it out to the crowd, but that is what I wanted to do. The chanting grew louder as the people responded to Republican candidate Donald Trump's mention of Hillary Clinton. "Lock her up. Lock her up!" The scene unfolded on the television screen. A chill passed through my body. The chant, the large group of people both angry and enthusiastic, reminded me of lynchings of the past.

Of course, lynchings were different. People were hung high, tarred and feathered, or beaten and burned. But the behavior begins in the same way. A crowd, angry at a seeming wrong, begins to hurl furious insults.

In a show of history repeating itself, I recently heard the same chant, but this time directed towards President Trump by a crowd at a campaign rally for Bernie Sanders: "Lock him up. Lock him up!"

This time of great political dissent and division rattles me. What if each of us tried to stop it? Could we step back, please?

I like to be right, it's true. Not my best quality, but one that I'm trying to rein in, particularly during political discussions. Maybe you're like me. Maybe you like to be right, too. But what if we're not? What if by listening to someone else we might discover an insight or a truth we hadn't thought of? Could we open ourselves up to that, or are we too determined to be right?

I remember a wise woman offering up this method of consideration when faced with a belief clearly different from her own. She'd say, "Why, I'd never thought about it in that way. I'll have to give that some more thought." Such a simple statement could relieve a moment of tension or build a bridge to communication. One's mind might even change!

Or how about another possibility of rethinking a position? Imagine taking a photo. Depending on where you stand, how you angle and zoom with the camera lens, your photo will turn out very differently. It's the same way with a reaction to a political candidate. Take some time and imagine yourself as a young black woman, or as a factory worker facing layoffs, or as a wealthy business owner. Then pause. Now take a look at the candidate. You may come up with a different picture each time.

I'm not suggesting that you change your mind; I'm suggesting that there are other ways to talk and think about our differences.

"Do You Vote?"

It was a momentous election – and I don't mean this one. The young pedicurist was busy at my feet, and I was wondering about what might be the outcome of the voting. "Do you vote?" I asked. She paused in her work and looked up at me, "I don't know how."

Don't know how? I was surprised. "You didn't learn how to do that in school?" Her response was, "Not that I remember." Later I asked my friend Joyce, "Did we learn about voting in school?" "Yes," said Joyce. "In third grade, Mrs. Qualley gave us a sample ballot and showed us how we could fill it out."

Now we're into another momentous election, and "Do You Vote?" has become my new question. It can be a simple way into talking to people about the power of the vote, and a quiet way into what can be the morass of mixed and passionate opinions.

I started asking the question because I was surprised by the number of people who said, "I don't talk politics with family or friends." Don't talk politics with family or friends? I thought of the old social adage, “Don’t talk about religion, politics, or money.” These are the topics that define us – our values, attitudes, and actions. They can determine how and where we live. Are we trying to just keep the conversation light and not go deeper? What are we missing if we avoid these topics?

I’ve asked that question – “Do you vote?” – probably a dozen times now, and I’ve never gotten the same answer. Sometimes I dig deeper – sometimes I don’t. It depends on the situation and the time.

My first foray into the question was when I was checking out of a hotel on my way home from a trip to Canada. Kamala Harris had just accepted the nomination to be the Democratic candidate for President after President Joe Biden had stepped aside. The young black receptionist was making morning greetings as she handled my payment when I asked, “Do you vote?” She looked at me in surprise, a smile lit her face, and she said, “Yes. Now I do.”

Waiting outside for the shuttle to the airport, I chatted with an elegantly dressed older woman. She’d been visiting family and was eager to get back home to New York. “Do you vote?” I asked. She said, “Oh, I mostly do. I just don't know if it makes any difference – if it counts." Hmm, I thought. I learned recently that the past Presidential election was decided by the equivalent of 2 votes per precinct. Clearly your vote counts – particularly in local elections or if you live in a swing state.

I thought of my conversation with a colleague. When I asked her if she voted, she said, "Yes! I taught civics. I told my students, 'You don't always have a voice. When you do, use it!'"

One day I saw two young men in a park hooking the flag in the back of their pickup to the top of a pole. I figured I knew which way they leaned in the Presidential campaign.

"Good morning," I called out as I approached them. "I was wondering – Do you vote?" They looked at each other and then at me, "No, we're too young." "Oh, how old are you?" "17." "Well, next year you can vote," I said, and then "I like your flag!" I had to chide myself as I walked away, "Stereotyping, aren't you?"

A new acquaintance I'd met – a 90- year-old woman who could nearly outpace me while walking – offered another take on voting. "Do you vote?" I asked.

"Oh, my husband and I were staunch Republicans – we *always* voted the ticket. But I just can't bring myself to vote for Trump."

"Will you vote for Harris?" She looked up at me, smiled, and said, "I'm working on it."

And then I asked the manicurist – a heavily tattooed young woman, "Do you vote?" "I can't," she said. Can't? I thought. Is she too young? I must have had a questioning look on my face because she said, "I have a felony. I have to wait 10 years – I have 2 more to go."

Interesting, I thought. Here we have a Presidential candidate with 34 felonies and he can vote, but she can't.

When I want to learn more, I've learned to ask, "What are you thinking?" It's a way to begin a conversation without bias or blame. And then I listen.

At minimum, during this momentous election, we need people to vote. And while at maximum, I would like to sway people to vote my way, I'll reserve conversation until I first hear if they vote and what they're thinking. It's the only way to start to find common ground.

I suggest that you start asking, "Do you vote?". Then listen.

Dig Deep

It hung for decades in the farmhouse kitchen where I grew up – a wooden plate sculpted with a harvest of fruits and vegetables encircling the words, "In Everything Give Thanks." (1 Thessalonians 5:18) Like many a wall hanging, it went without notice except when a visitor might occasionally spot it and comment, or when we'd glance up and see it as our gaze turned out the window. But quiet though it was, it did its magic. It seeped into my system.

Now it hangs above my own kitchen sink and I notice it more often. Sometimes I think, "*Really?* In *Everything* Give Thanks?" But perhaps because I'm growing older, or because it reminds me of cherished wisdom from my parents, I pause to take it in. I'm helped enormously by recognizing it doesn't say "*For* Everything Give Thanks," but instead "*In* Everything Give Thanks." It instructs me that, on occasion, I must dig deep.

Giving thanks doesn't always come fast or first, certainly not in the case of tough news. Thanks can be late in arriving. Other emotions rise to the forefront –

frustration, dismay, anger. And sometimes those emotions don't ever go away, but they're tempered by time and the search for acceptance and gratitude.

In some of life's circumstances, it's often much easier when you're looking back to see reasons for thanks. For example, the job I resigned from under duress brought me to another "best job ever." Or my beloved country retreat, claimed by the government for flood control that resulted in a buyout, eventually gave me hope for a new outdoor retreat.

The recent election catapulted me into a cauldron of emotions. As an independent but left-leaning voter, I was actually speechless at the results. Which was fortunate because it gave me time to absorb and think. I couldn't understand how a person who lacked the character traits necessary for a good leader could possibly be elected.

I know it's a troubled and divisive time, but since quite a number of people whom I really like voted for President-elect Trump, I needed to reconcile my thoughts and future actions. How was I to do this?

In situations not to your liking, a good exercise for mental health is the attempt to dig deep to find some tiny ray of hope. It doesn't always work and may not work quickly, but it can be kind of rewarding – and a way to sidestep disappointment or despair. Bottom line is that you're not going to change the circumstances, but the aim is to change yourself or your perspective.

I tried that with the results of the election. It took a few days, but then I actually found some relief and a reason or two to give thanks. At least, we won't have to wade through two months of this election being called fraudulent or rigged. We won't have to survive another call to take over the capital, with injuries and deaths resulting. For me, small mercies, but at least for the moment – and this moment is truly all that we ever have – these are reasons to give thanks. Most importantly, reasons to help ground me.

Grounding is what it's all about. Joyce Sequilchie Hifler in her book, *A Cherokee Feast of Days*, says, "Whatever is loudest gets our attention, and all that delights and comforts slips by without our seeing it." I've learned to be diligent and disciplined – in the midst of what is "loud" – to find moments to see and cherish.

Oftentimes those moments for me happen outdoors. The November sky is spectacular with stars. I step out on my balcony in the early morning hours and gaze in awe at the grandeur above me. In the daylight, the carpet of golden leaves covering the ground is a call to beauty and comfort.

I recall the day my niece, a teacher, was involved in a horrific school shooting. The echoes of the sounds associated with that event – and the impact on her and others – played loud in my brain. I wrapped myself in a blanket and sat on a bench on my balcony, seeking solace. Cardinals are beautiful songbirds, yet I've never seen them around my home. That day, as I sat in sorrow, a bright red cardinal landed and sat on the railing. Peace landed in me too. I've never again seen a cardinal on my balcony.

Lifetimes on earth are short. "The days of our life are seventy years or perhaps eighty if we are strong . . . they are soon gone and we fly away." (Psalm 90:10) My brother died at 50 years of age, my sister at 60, and my husband at 74. While I have mourned those losses and dearly wish each one had lived longer, I try to honor and give thanks for their lifetime with me by having an open heart to gratitude. How do I do that? Dig deep, be still, and find all I can. . . in the people I meet and the situations I encounter. . . for which I can say "Thank you."

The pathway to peace is aiming to find in all events something of value or beauty. Something that gives us glimmers of hope. Over time, this practice builds a storehouse of touchstones that we can return to again and again for grounding and for gratitude.

Deciding to Bend (Perhaps)

By Mark Bratlie

I think I will make a decision today
 Yes, that's the thing to do
I will plant my feet on solid ground
 And set them in concrete too
Then I will know right where I am at
 While others praise my resolve
I will stand as a giant redwood tree
 With my posture straight and tall

Enough of wishy-washy-ness
 And changes of my mind
Perhaps this and maybe that
 And conclusions not on time
Consideration of other perspectives
 Can seem like a sputtering plan
Much better it is to be resolute
 Standing tall and proud like a man

But then again (yes, I knew it would happen)
  Perhaps I decide with haste
Surely there are things to be said
  For a slower more flexible pace
We tend to admire the hard and fast
  And the will independent and strong
Even though the preformed opinion
  Quite often ends up to be wrong

I would rather take some time (not wasted)
  To view multiple variables
While letting go of fast-hard-rightness
  And other illusory fables
To pause in front of action
  Is hardly a weak waste of time
Being open to measured deliberation
  Is a fine use of this human mind

True strength need not be characterized
  As stiff and hard and unbending
Consider the sapling in heavy wind

  As it sways and gives way without breaking
Pausing to listen is also not weakness
  And resoluteness is not always strong
Being open to questions is not wishy-washy
  While indecision is not always wrong (I think)

CHAPTER 11

A New Beginning

Shirley's Prayer

My sister Shirley's solo visits to me were rare. Often when we gathered, other family members were present – her husband Al, her daughters Jill and Karen, our parents, or other relatives or friends.

But I cherished the solo visits because they meant more time for us to be alone, more things to do that both of us enjoyed. We took in realtors' open-house tours, quilt shows, fabric stores, and thrift shops. We drove, we walked, and we talked.

It's intriguing to me how, after a dear one like my sister Shirley passes, small details show up in vivid relief. Almost like a painting, where certain colors jump out at you and remain a bright point of your remembrance.

On one of her last solo visits with me, Shirley and I sat on high stools at the breakfast nook in my small kitchen. Grape Nuts cereal, skim milk, yogurt, and a banana awaited us.

Shirley was a prayer person, and so before we began, she bowed her head, gathered her hands, closed her eyes, and spoke:

> "We thank you for the morning light,
> for rest and shelter of the night,
> for food, family, and friends,
> for everything Thy goodness sends. Amen."

Her voice was strong. The prayer was new to me.

Later, I learned the prayer was written by Ralph Waldo Emerson. But ever since I told the story of Shirley's last visit and her breakfast prayer – how I could still hear her saying it – how it said everything one would want to say in thanks – our family has adopted it as our own. We use it morning, noon, or night. We call it The Shirley Prayer.

Shine Before You Rise

Many years ago, a local columnist, who was prone to late night hours and who had to drag herself out of bed in the morning, told this story of her eight-year-old daughter. Upon being wakened by her worn and weary mother, the little girl exclaimed, "Oh good! It's time to start a new day."

I was deeply touched by the story of this young girl's joy in greeting the morning. Sometime after that, and facing a stressful type of day myself, I decided that I might need to incorporate her kind of gladness into the hours ahead of me. It was not easy, but I was tired of muddling through my waking hours, and I wanted a new focus that would provide some propulsion into the day. And so, I began.

Little by little, it has become a ritual for me. Before rising from my bed, I greet the day with gladness and thanks. Sometimes I even manage to amuse myself. This morning I struggled awake from some dreams, and then with a little impromptu melody I sang out, "Oh yes, I get to see a new day… Alleluia!" The tune that rang out from my heart surprised me, and I chuckled out loud.

When I told this story to a friend, she remarked, "Well, you must be a morning person." The idea that, before putting one's feet on the floor, one would call out a greeting to the day seemed highly suspect to her. I admitted to her that my tune of joy wasn't totally natural — on any number of days, I have to work hard to get up to it.

It's a bit like you'd warm up your voice before singing in public. I often get some false starts and have to begin again. But I'm determined not to let my feet hit the floor until I've accomplished this morning task of thanks.

I guess you could look at it from two perspectives. One is that it is a rather bizarre way to rise up in the morning. The other is that it is the best way to rise up in the morning. I've come to believe in both.

Let's face it. The world we know can be startling in its changes, turmoil, grief, and stress. I know those themes are a given in our world, but I want thankfulness to be another. The richness of a thankful heart brings a balm and a blessing to every kind of situation.

The poet Mary Oliver, in her book of essays and other writings called *Long Life*, wrote: "Here you are, alive. Would you like to make a comment?"

Yes, I would, and my comment is: "*Shine before you rise...with thanks.*"

Morning's Light

By Mark Bratlie

The break of day…what a misnomer.
    It does not break…it spreads all over –
Over the trees and the dewy leaves,
    Over the branches as early light dances.

Over the clouds and through the sky,
    Morning's beauty brings tears to my eyes.
Over the birds and over the bees,
    Exposing colors for eyes to see.

From muted shades to glorious hues,
    Morning's light serves as a mystic muse.
My eyes feast on an expanding bouquet
    As I witness the birth of a glorious day.

This show that humans could never create
    Leads me to delight and a humble state.
I know how blessed and grateful I am
    Since this show I'll enjoy again and again.

Credits

ANDERSON, JEAN. "A Good Man," *Northern Narratives*, FARGO PUBLIC LIBRARY, 2024.

BRATLIE, MARK. "A Falling Leaf," *Northern Narratives*, FARGO PUBLIC LIBRARY, 2020.

BRATLIE, MARK. "Prairie Spirit," *Northern Narratives*, FARGO PUBLIC LIBRARY, 2019.

HIFLER, JOYCE. "April 25 - Page 133." *Cherokee Feast of Days: Daily Meditations*, COUNCIL OAKS DISTRIBUTION, 2018.

OLIVER, MARY. *Long Life: Essays and Other Writings.* CAMBRIDGE, MA: DA CAPO PRESS, 2004.

VEYLANSWAMI, SATGURU BODHINATHA. *A Character Building Workbook - 64 Qualities to help build, transform and improve life.* HIMALAYAN ACADEMY, 2015.

With Thanks

We think of writing as a solo activity – which it is – but it's not without the involvement of other people! The pages of this book have the fingerprints of many: the friends, family, and strangers who brought their lives to the pages, the colleagues who did first readings and made critical suggestions, the professionals who have editing skills that help turn an okay paragraph into a really good passage, and the experts who can navigate the digital world with finesse.

With thanks to my first readers: the Scribes writing group, Marian Zieske, Sheri Fercho, Bea Kinzler, and Dianna Hatfield Clemenson. And to my friend from the 1960s and beyond, Colleen Myers, who helped me create the flow for the book; she also introduced me to the flow of yin yoga. Their critical feedback plus encouragement moved me forward and made me want to carry on.

To my super editor and colleague from my first writing group: Charlotte Cox. Together, over a weekend in New Hampshire, plus countless hours over the phone, we commiserated, chatted, and challenged each other as we made our way through my essays and Mark's poems. Charlotte's career as an editor provided critical corrections and guidance, and it has made the book into the best it could be. Also, due for applause as cheerleader and editor is Marlene Johnson. There's nothing like a communications coach and a lover of theater to help shape concepts into sharp and cogent focus. Both women stood by my side as I made my way to the completion of *All That Matters.*

Two people stand out for their creativity and tech savviness: Lonna Whiting, who helped create my website – jean-anderson.net – which has served as a jump-off point for launching my essays; and Loralee Meier, a whiz and a wonder with all things digital.

Finally, to my friends, family, and readers who have shared thoughtful reflections and insights on my essays and Mark's poems – thank you all!

Made in USA - Kendallville, IN
72598_9798284521014
10.21.2025 0228